OTHER DIMENSIONS

Exploring The Unexplained

Michio Kushi
with Edward Esko

AVERY PUBLISHING GROUP INC.

Garden City Park, New York

The health procedures in this book are based on the training, personal experiences, and research of the authors. Because each person and situation is unique, the editor and the publisher urge the reader to check with a qualified health professional before using any procedure where there is any question as to its appropriateness. The publisher does not advocate the use of any particular diet, but believes the information presented in this book should be available to the public.

Cover design: Rudy Shur and Janine Eisner-Wall
In-house editor: Elaine Will Sparber
Typesetting: Pro-To-Type Unlimited

Library of Congress Cataloging-in-Publication Data

Kushi, Michio.
  Other dimensions : exploring the unexplained / Michio Kushi with
Edward Esko.
    p. cm.
  Includes bibliographical references and index.
  ISBN 0-89529-450-8
  1. Occultism. 2. Reincarnation. 3. Unidentified flying objects.
4. Macrobiotic diet—Miscellanea. I. Esko, Edward. II. Title.
BF1439.K87 1992
133—dc20   90-21725
                                            CIP

Printed in the United States of America

10   9   8   7   6   5   4   3   2

Contents

Introduction

Part of the beauty of macrobiotic philosophy is the ease with which it embraces and explains the endless variety of ways that human beings perceive reality. It encourages holistic, non-exclusive modes of thought that are based on the unity between ancient and modern, spiritual and scientific, and Eastern and Western views of the world and challenges each of us to mobilize our left-brain powers of analysis in addition to our right-brain capacities for intuitive understanding and insight. Whether or not we are able to pass through the ongoing crisis posed by modern technology and enter an era of health, peace, and ecological harmony may well depend on our ability to think and act with truly holistic, non-dogmatic flexibility.

In this book, we discuss a variety of fascinating and timely issues, including UFOs and extraterrestrials, Oriental medicine, alchemy, ghosts, reincarnation, and prophecies and predictions—as well as timeless questions of spiritual origin and destiny—in light of the macrobiotic cosmology of endless change. The ideas in this book challenge and expand the frontiers of modern knowledge. We encourage you to approach them in the spirit of *non-credo*; that is, not to believe or accept them without thinking, but to arrive at conclusions based on your own insights and experience.

Although each of these topics is of contemporary interest, all have been discussed since ancient times. The Bible, the *Vedas*, the *Kojiki*, and other ancient texts contain numerous accounts that can plausibly be interpreted as referring to encounters with extraterrestrial beings. These are reviewed in Chapter 1, along with a variety of modern ideas about UFOs. The medical systems of ancient China, India, Japan, and Greece were based on an understanding of the body's energy system and utilized healing techniques such as acupuncture, massage, and herbal medicine that attempted to restore energy balance. They also shared a fundamental belief in balanced diet as a primary means of achieving health. These approaches are reviewed in Chapter 2 and are explained in terms of the macrobiotic understanding of *yin* and *yang* and *ki* energy.

Alchemy, which we discuss in Chapter 3, has its origin in the cosmology of change underlying all great spiritual and philosophical teachings and was practiced widely in the ancient world, laying the foundation for the modern development of chemistry and physics. This ancient art was revived in the twentieth century by George Ohsawa and his associates, and in the chapter on alchemy, we review Ohsawa's experiments and discuss their implications for the future.

Discussions of life after death, reincarnation, and the spiritual world are common to all people in all times and are found in all the world's great spiritual and philosophical traditions, as is an understanding of the role that a diet of whole grains and vegetables plays in the development of consciousness and spirituality. These issues are reviewed in Chapter 4 and are explained in terms of the spiral structure of the material and spiritual worlds. Throughout the centuries, prophets and thinkers such as Isaiah, Nostradamus, Toynbee, and Edgar Cayce have made predictions concerning our modern era—including the current transition from a material to a spiritual civilization—based on their understanding of the law of change and an awareness of the celestial cycles that govern human events. These cycles are explained in the concluding chapter and form the basis for the predictions presented in that section.

Even with the development of science and technology over the past several centuries, many of life's most basic questions remain unsolved. Questions such as why we have five fingers and five toes,why there is an ocean at the North Pole and a continent at the South Pole, why there are so few green flowers, what is memory and where it exists, and many others await satisfactory answers. It is our hope that *Other Dimensions* will stimulate new ways of thinking about some of life's most basic mysteries—along with fresh new approaches to health, ecology, and world peace—while rekindling everyone's sense of wonder and marvel at the vast order of the universe, of which human beings on Earth are but a small part. This revolution in consciousness complements the revolution in diet and health that macrobiotic education has pioneered over the past thirty years throughout the world.

We would like to thank everyone who contributed to this book. We thank Rudy Shur and Elaine Will Sparber of Avery Publishing Group for their guidance and assistance, along with Alex Jack for providing research and statistics used in the text. We also thank the staff members of *Order of the Universe* magazine, where some of this material was published in the past, for their editorial and production assistance.

Michio Kushi
Edward Esko
Becket, Massachusetts

OTHER DIMENSIONS

1.

Extraterrestrial Encounters

As a scientist, I must be mindful of the lessons of the past; all too often it has happened that matters of great value to science were overlooked because the new phenomenon simply did not fit the accepted scientific outlook of the time.

> J. Allen Hyneck
> UFO Investigator
> Project Blue Book

A long time ago, a young man from America set out to travel the world. In the course of his travels, he visited Istanbul, where he fell in love with a beautiful young princess. Unfortunately for the two lovers, the girl's parents opposed the idea of marriage to a young foreigner, and so the romance had to come to an end.

On the day the young man was to depart from Istanbul, the princess took him to the treasury room of the Topkapi palace. There she opened a large case filled with sapphires, rubies, gold, and many precious ornaments, and she told him, "Pick out one treasure to take with you, so you will always have something to remember me by." The young man thought to himself, "If I take some valuable piece of jewelry or gold, that would be too selfish," so he picked up a very old scroll and said, "I'd like to have this." Immediately, the girl went pale. She told him, "Please don't take that. There is a very old, strange story about that document; anyone who possesses it will suffer a terrible fate. It has been kept in secret for hundreds of years, and nobody knows how old it really is." But since the young man insisted, she let him take it. Naturally, he couldn't understand what it said, so he eventually gave it to a naval officer he met who kept it stored away for a long time.

The scroll was discovered again in 1952 and sent to a team of scholars for examination. The scholars found that it was a map drafted in the year 1513 by a Turkish admiral named Piri Reis. According to the inscriptions in Latin and Turkish, it was a compilation of twenty older maps dating back at least 2,000 years. The map was very detailed and seemed to contain the outline of several continents, including North and South America, Africa, and Antarctica. But even more astonishing was the fact that the continental South Pole, with all its bays and mountains buried beneath the ice, was also clearly outlined. Modern cartographers had only recently discovered many of the South Pole's topographical features—yet here they were on a clearly drawn map dating from several thousand years ago.

There was one still stranger fact. Despite the accuracy of all the continental outlines, the map's perspective was slightly unusual: the Southern Hemisphere appeared a little larger than normal, and the Northern Hemisphere a little smaller, as if the map had been composed from an odd angle. Then the cartographers compared the map with modern satellite photos—the proportions were identical. The old map had been set down in the manner of an aerial photograph taken from far above the Earth. How could ancient people have seen the world from this perspective? The answer to this question remains a mystery.

Several years before World War II, an international team of scientists, scholars, and university students went into the Yucatan on an expedition to explore Mayan ruins. One day, in the village of Palenque, they came to a large, ruined temple, which was overgrown with trees and vines. They cut through the foliage and made their way into the temple, then traveled through long passageways and finally arrived at the central chamber. After many hours of work, they succeeded in prying open the great stone door, and they turned their flashlights on a large stone coffin. One of the female students suddenly screamed; the other team members rushed over. "What happened?" they asked.

There on the coffin's surface, illuminated by the young woman's flashlight, was a large engraving of an ancient Mayan operating some type of complicated machine surrounded by stars. What seemed to be flames were shooting out of the front and back of the strange apparatus, and an array of complicated dials, levers, and other devices was depicted on its inside. The engraving was at least 2,000 years old, and at the time of its discovery, no one could figure out what it meant. It wasn't until the launching of manned space vehicles more than a generation later that a possible explanation was proposed. Perhaps the engraving was a picture of an ancient Indian operating some type of space vehicle. If this theory is correct, ancient people may have used, or at least known about, rockets and space travel.

Throughout the world, there have been many similar discoveries, revealing evidence that ancient man may have witnessed episodes far beyond our present understanding. These discoveries point to the intriguing possibilities that our ancient ancestors were visited by people with a highly advanced technology and that these visitors came by space travel from beyond the planet Earth.

WHEELS OF FIRE

Together with this pictorial type of evidence, there are also very interesting stories within ancient legends and historical documents. In the Tigris-Euphrates river valley, located in what is now Iraq, the Sumerian culture emerged. According to archeologists, this is the cradle of human civilization. Sumer is older than any society in the Western Hemisphere. It is older than the civilization of Egypt, and it predates Chinese history. Portions of engraved clay tablets from early Sumeria chronicle a scenario of gods flying in the sky, of these gods landing and teaching the Sumerians new ways of life. Some of the descriptions are metaphorical; others are literal.

Records of similar encounters exist in ancient writings and mythologies from elsewhere around the world. Indian, Chinese, Mayan, and Egyptian legends speak of encounters with mysterious flying machines. An ancient Sanskrit text known as the *Drona Parva* describes gods piloting aerial vehicles known as *vimanas*. The Bible also contains a number of passages that could be interpreted as records of extraterrestrial encounters. Genesis, chapter 6, records what may have been one of these encounters:

> And it came to pass, when men began to multiply on the face of the earth, and daughters were born unto them, that the sons of God saw the daughters of men that they were fair; and they took them wives of all which they chose. . . . There were giants in the earth in those days; and also after that, when the sons of God came in unto the daughters of men, and they bare children to them, the same became mighty men which were of old, men of renown.

Beings from another world may have visited the Earth, mingled with the human race, and left descendants that are still among us. In another well-known Biblical passage, taken from the Old Testament book that bears his name, the prophet Ezekiel, a priest in one of Babylon's captive Jewish settlements, records what may have been an encounter with one or more flying ships from space:

> Now it came to pass . . . as I was among the captives by the river of Chebar, that the heavens were opened, and I saw visions of God. . . . And I looked, and, behold, a whirlwind came out of the north, a great cloud, and a fire infolding itself, and a brightness was about it, and out of the midst thereof as the colour of amber, out of the midst of the fire. Also out of the midst thereof came the likeness of four living creatures. And this was their appearance; they had the likeness of a man. And every one had four faces, and every one had four wings. And their feet were straight feet; and the sole of their feet was like the sole of a calf's foot: and they sparkled like the colour of burnished brass. . . .
> Now as I beheld the living creatures, behold one wheel upon the earth by the living creatures, with his four faces. The appearance of the wheels and their work was like unto the colour of a beryl: and they four had

one likeness: and their appearance and their work was as it were a wheel in the middle of a wheel. When they went, they went upon their four sides: and they turned not when they went. As for their rings, they were so high that they were dreadful; and their rings were full of eyes round about them four. And when the living creatures went, the wheels went by them: and when the living creatures were lifted up from the earth, the wheels were lifted up.

These flying ships may have utilized *ki*, or electromagnetic energy, as their primary power source. Ezekiel describes their movements as being guided by some type of invisible energy or spirit:

Whithersoever the spirit was to go, they went. . . . And when they went, I heard the noise of their wings, like the noise of great waters, as the voice of the Almighty, the voice of speech, as the noise of an host: when they stood, they let down their wings.

THE AGE OF THE GODS

Ancient documents in Japan offer some of the world's most fascinating and revealing accounts of flying machines, extraterrestrial encounters, and visitations by gods from beyond the Earth. Two of them are well-known historical documents. The first is called *Kojiki*, or "Record of Old Events." It is said to chronicle the beginning of Japan. The other Japanese historical record is called *Nihon Shoki*. "Nihon" is the Japanese name for Japan itself, composed of the words for "sun" and "origin"—in other words, Japan is the "Sun Origin Country." Some people interpret this to mean that Japan was originally founded by people who came from the Sun.

Both documents contain similar histories. They describe Japan as beginning with the so-called "age of the gods," when various god-like men and women descended from a place called Takama, which literally means "high heavenly field" or "heavenly place." When the gods (they are described by different names) saw that the Earth was ready, they descended to the Earth to the mountain Takachiho. From there, they spread and settled throughout the Earth.

The description of the age of the gods is followed in both these texts by a history of the present dynasty, beginning with the emperor Jinmu. According to both stories, Jinmu gathered his people together and said, "Our purpose in coming down to this land was to bring peace to this world. Our ancestors first came here many thousands of years ago, yet we still have not accomplished this task. I have heard from a very wise man that a long time ago, a god named Nin-Hayashi descended to the mountain of Kushi-Fu-Taki. This place is very beautiful, so let us go there to join his descendants and work together with them."

According to the legend, Jinmu and his people traveled to join Nin-Hayashi's descendants, who were at that time called *Kushi-Nin-Hayashi*. When they arrived, the two clans of heavenly-descended people recognized that they had both come from the same place, and together they created a new capital, which became the beginning of what is now called Nihon, or Japan.

That area, located on the Sea of Japan, is now called Izumo. There is an old shrine there, dating from ancient times. Within this shrine is a smaller shrine that is dedicated to *kama*, the old-style wooden pot used for cooking rice. According to an old story, a man came riding down from heaven a long time ago in a special type of ship. To remember his teachings, the people made a replica of that special ship and enshrined it. The old-fashioned rice pot, or kama, and the flying machine were apparently of a similar design.

In another set of documents, known as the *Kogu-Shuri*, or "Collection of Ancient Words," there is an account of gods from other planets bringing the first grains of rice to Earth. According to that story, rice grew on a heavenly planet and was brought to Earth to ensure health, peace, and prosperity among the people. Native Americans have similar legends about the origin of corn. And the ancient Greeks believed that civilization began with the use of cereal grains. According to Greek legend, the goddess Demeter (renamed Ceres by the Romans) gave the first seeds of wheat to her priest, Triptolemus, and instructed him to fly around the Earth in a fiery chariot to bring grains of this wheat, and the blessings of agriculture and civilization, to all people. Other Japanese legends credit gods from other planets with bringing a number of additional "treasures" to Earth, including the solar and lunar calendars, a knowledge of natural healing, techniques of pyramid construction, and a universal cosmology based on the interplay of two complementary energies.

Another set of ancient Japanese documents, known as the *Isohara* or *Takeuchi Scrolls*, contains maps like those found in the Topkapi palace. One of these maps is thought to have been originally composed more than 12,000 years ago. This ancient drawing depicts the continents of North and South America, along with Greenland, Africa, Australia, and Eurasia. Each continent has a name, written in ancient language. North America, for example, is called Ebirisu-Hinata, which means "Country That Receives the Sun." South America is referred to as Ebirisu-Hiuke, or "Country Where the Sun Directly Shines." But even more intriguing is the presence of two large continents in the mid-Pacific. One, located to the north, is called Miyoi, and the other, more to the south, is called Tamiara. These are the so-called lost continents of Mu, which, according to the English scholar James Churchward, contained an advanced civilization that disappeared before the dawn of recorded history. Equally fascinating is the presence of a land mass in the area between North and South America in the region that is now the Caribbean. This land mass corresponds to the lost continent of Atlantis.

The Isohara documents include a second map that according to the text was composed more than 6,000 years after the first one. In this more recent drawing, the continents in the Pacific are missing, as is the land mass in the Caribbean. In their place is an ancient word that means "sunk." The texts that accompany the maps talk about an ancient world civilization in which global communication and transportation, including by flying machine, were common, as was contact with visitors from space.

PYRAMIDS AND STONE CIRCLES

Ten miles west of Cairo, the Great Pyramid of Cheops rises with dramatic suddenness above the rocky Giza plateau. This single immense structure covers a ground area of over thirteen acres and is composed of some 2.3 million limestone blocks that weigh an average of two and a half tons each. The Great Pyramid and two smaller ones nearby were built during Egypt's fourth dynasty, between 2613 and 2494 B.C. For centuries, people have been speculating that the Great Pyramid is more than just a burial place for the pharaoh Cheops. Could this ancient enigma be part of a global network of similar structures?

In several places throughout Japan are mysterious standing stones that were put into position many thousands of years ago. Like the megaliths of Stonehenge, these giant rocks were transported over great distances. Their purpose remains a mystery. Many of them have ancient engravings on their surface, including drawings of spirals, stars, and constellations.

One mysterious group of stones is located in the northern part of Honshu, the main island of Japan, on top of a volcanic mountain with a beautiful lake at its summit. Of the two stones in this structure, one lies flat and the other is positioned vertically. The stones are positioned in perfect alignment with the Earth's north-south axis.

The local people say that the mountain has mysterious power, similar to that attributed to Mount Shasta in California. According to legend, evil-minded people who climb the mountain are overcome with a strange, mysterious illness, while pure-minded people feel energized and elevated after climbing it. Over the centuries, there have also been reports of strange lights and flying objects in the vicinity of the mountain. As a result of these occurrences, the local people refer to the mountain as a "magic mountain" or "mountain of the gods."

When viewed from a distance, the mountain has an almost perfectly symmetrical shape that resembles the shape of a pyramid, and its legend states that at one time this is exactly what it was. According to the story, the ancient manmade structure exploded and triggered a volcanic eruption that released tons of lava and molten rock. The pyramid was completely covered and now resembles a large, inactive volcano similar to Mount Fuji.

The Wyoming Medicine Wheel

Mysterious stone circles have been found throughout North America that like Stonehenge and other megalithic sites in Europe may have been used as astronomical observatories. One of these ancient wheels is located in Wyoming, high in the Bighorn mountains.

Known as the Bighorn medicine wheel, this stone circle is over eighty feet in diameter. Radiating out from a central hub of stones are numerous spokes that connect to an outer wheel, or rim. Small piles of stones, or cairns, are positioned in the center and around the outer circle.

Observers have discovered numerous alignments between the rocks and celestial bodies. For example, two of the cairns mark the rising and setting of the Sun at the summer solstice. Other stones point to the rising and setting of certain other stars during seasonal changes.

Archeologists are uncertain as to the exact purpose of the Bighorn wheel and similar structures. However, it is possible that they were part of a network of similar structures found throughout the world and represent traces of an ancient cosmology inherited from visitors from space.

Similar sites have been found on Hokkaido, the northernmost island of Japan, and on the southern island of Kyushu. If we draw a line due west from the site in Kyushu, it crosses a region deep within the remote desert of western China, where a pyramid larger and possibly older than the Great Pyramid has been discovered. If we continue west in a straight line, we arrive at the Great Pyramid of Cheops. Could it be that pyramids, stone circles, and similar ancient structures were erected as part of a world-scale plan? If this is the case, then how did ancient man gain the ability to devise a plan of such enormity?

FLYING SAUCERS

Several years ago, my wife Aveline and I gave some macrobiotic seminars in Venezuela. While waiting at the Caracas airport for our flight back to Boston, an announcement suddenly
came over the public address system: "Two unidentified flying
objects have been spotted on radar hovering several thousand
feet above the airport. Please wait for further information."
Needless to say, the airport burst into pandemonium. Within
minutes, a second announcement reported that the objects had
"accelerated to a tremendous speed and were no longer visible
on radar."

Mysterious flying objects have been reported since the beginning of history. In 329 B.C., the army of Alexander the Great
was reported to have been harassed by several flying machines.
In the 1500s, numerous spheres and disks were reported in the
skies over Nuremberg, Germany, and Basel, Switzerland. Even
the future King George V of England as a young man in the
summer of 1881 saw what appeared to be a flying ship off the
coast of Australia. Sightings such as these of unidentified flying
objects (UFOs) continued into the early part of this century and
through World War II. The modern UFO era is said to have
begun on June 24, 1947, when an amateur pilot named Kenneth
Arnold spotted a formation of flying objects gliding over the
Cascade Mountains in Washington State while he was flying
his small private plane. Arnold calculated that the UFOs were
flying at no less than 1,350 miles per hour, much faster than any
known aircraft. When asked to describe their flight pattern, he
said, "They flew like a saucer would if you skipped it across
the water." With Arnold's description, the era of "flying
saucers" began.

Since then, sightings of flying saucers have tended to occur
in waves, with the number of reports peaking in certain years
and leveling off in others. During the wave of sightings that occurred in 1952, there were more than 1,500 reports of UFOs in
North America alone. The majority of these sightings were
made by ordinary people on the ground; others were made by
professional pilots in flight, both with and without radar con-
firmation. As the flying saucer era continued, new dimensions
were added by stories describing the actual sighting of aliens,

followed by stories in which people claimed to be abducted by visitors from space.

From the beginning, modern UFO reports have generated a great deal of scientific controversy and skepticism. In the late 1940s, the United States Air Force launched an official probe into these sightings that was eventually given the code name Project Blue Book. J. Allen Hyneck, a professor of astronomy at Ohio State University, was chosen by the Air Force to evaluate the reports from a scientific perspective.

Like many of his scientific colleagues, Hyneck seriously doubted that UFOs were real. However, after looking into the reports for nearly twenty years, his opinion started to change. Hyneck told a congressional committee investigating UFOs in 1966 that the official policy had always been to assume that UFOs were not real and "that a conventional explanation existed, either as a misidentification or as an otherwise well known object or phenomenon, a hallucination, or a hoax." However, he stated, although the majority of sightings fit that description, a small minority defied scientific explanation. At a congressional hearing held several years later, Hyneck explained why his opinion had changed and called for a more thorough investigation of the UFO phenomenon due to "the cumulative weight of continued reports from groups of people around the world whose competence and sanity I have no reason to doubt, reports involving unexplainable craft with physical effects on animals, motor vehicles, growing plants, and on the ground."

Nevertheless, Project Blue Book was discontinued in 1969 following the release of a controversial report prepared by a committee at the University of Colorado chaired by Edward Condon, a prominent physicist. The Condon committee concluded, "Nothing has come from the study of UFOs in the past 21 years that has added to scientific knowledge. Careful consideration of the record leads us to conclude that further extensive study of UFOs probably cannot be justified. . . ." However, critics pointed out that this conclusion was arrived at even though 30 percent of the cases analyzed by the Condon committee remained unsolved, a figure that was substantially higher than the official Project Blue Book classification of about 5 percent of reported sightings as "unidentified." Critics also questioned the objectivity of the report, claiming that Professor Condon had already been biased against UFOs before the committee even began to review the evidence.

Although the Condon report led to the demise of the official government investigation of UFOs, it did not slow the number of sightings reported around the world. One well-publicized sighting occurred in the fall of 1969 when Governor Jimmy Carter and about a dozen other people saw a bright object about the size of the Moon in the night sky over Georgia. The object hovered motionless and also moved back and forth before disappearing. Carter reported the object as a UFO and, when he became president, encouraged the National Aeronautics and Space Administration (NASA) to begin a thorough study of UFOs.

Meanwhile, public fascination with unidentified flying objects has continued to the present, with the recent Soviet report of a spaceship landing in the Caucasus as a case in point. A Gallup poll taken in 1987 revealed that 49 percent of Americans

Close Encounters

The term close encounters *was coined by investigator J. Allen Hyneck in his 1972 book,* The UFO Experience. *In the book, Hyneck classifies UFO sightings into six categories. Sightings made from a distance are organized into three categories: lights seen at night; flying disks seen during the day; and visual sightings confirmed by radar, such as those reported by amateur and professional pilots. Close encounters are sightings made at less than 500 feet. Those of the first kind involve only the sighting of an object. In those of the second kind, some type of physical evidence is left behind, including depressions in the ground caused by landing gear. A close encounter of the third kind is a close-up sighting of an alien being in or around a UFO.*

were convinced that UFOs were real, while an earlier survey had revealed that as many as one American in eleven—an estimated 13 million people—had actually seen a UFO.

WHERE DO THEY COME FROM?

Theories about the origin of UFOs are numerous. Several theories attribute their origin to the Earth rather than outer space. According to one idea, as World War II was ending, a group of Nazis escaped to Antarctica by submarine. They brought advanced rocket technology with them and established a secret base from which they periodically launch flying machines. However, this theory doesn't account for the ancient, historical sightings or for the many old legends about extraterrestrial encounters.

Another theory attributes the origin of UFOs to an advanced civilization living inside the Earth. This notion arose out of the so-called "hollow Earth theory," which has existed in one form or another since the beginning of the scientific era. Edmund Halley, the seventeenth-century English astronomer and discoverer of the comet that bears his name, believed that multiple planets exist within the Earth's interior, one inside the other. Later proponents of the hollow Earth theory believed that a single sun is at the center of the Earth and that human beings, possibly with an advanced civilization, are also inside the planet. This idea gained prominence during the nineteenth century and led the United States Navy to send several ships to explore Antarctica for an opening to the interior world. It also inspired novels such as Jules Verne's *Journey to the Center of the Earth*.

Ancient legends also spoke of an advanced civilization in the Earth's interior. According to the Lama sect of Buddhism, the kingdom at the center of the Earth is named Agartha and is inhabited by a race of spiritually advanced people, including descendants of the vanished civilizations of Mu and Atlantis. This subterranean civilization is linked by a network of tunnels that comes to the surface in places such as the Himalayas, Rockies, Andes, and other mountain ranges on the Earth. Some proponents use the hollow Earth theory to explain the sudden disappearance of the Incas and other ancient civilizations, believing that these lost people fled underground through secret passageways.

Nineteenth-century proponents of the hollow Earth theory believed that there are openings in both the North and South Poles that lead to the underground realm. These holes were believed to be inclined at such an angle that a person could wander into them without noticing it. Before long, the traveler would see a new sun, which is smaller and dimmer than our sun, along with oceans, land, mountains, and other features that resemble those on the surface of the Earth, including plants and animals. UFOs supposedly enter and leave the underground realm through these polar openings.

A completely different line of reasoning about the origin of UFOs is that they come from space but from within our own solar system. There are a variety of opinions within this general category, including that they come from Mars, Venus, and other nearby planets; that they originally came from a planet that was destroyed long ago, either through nuclear war or a natural catastrophe; and that they come from an as-yet-undiscovered planet. We will consider each of these opinions next, beginning with the idea that UFOs originate on our neighboring planets.

A SPIRAL MODEL OF THE SOLAR SYSTEM

According to present estimates, the surface temperature of Mercury is about 340°C. (644°F.) during the daytime and about –120°C. (–184°F.) at night. With such extremes of temperature, it is thought that life cannot exist on this first planet out from the Sun. Venus, the next planet out from the Sun, is generally assumed to be too hot to support life, although recent data indicate that the temperature beneath its thick atmosphere may not be as high as was previously thought. Given these conditions, it is difficult to explain certain ancient legends saying that a long time ago, people from Venus came to Earth in several waves of flying ships. Is it possible that conditions on Venus, and perhaps on Mercury as well, were at one time more conducive to life than they seem to be at present?

In order to evaluate these legends, we need a model of the solar system that is more dynamic than the one currently proposed by science. Nothing in this universe is absolutely constant or identical. Our common sense tells us that everything changes. Therefore, the position of the planets relative to the Sun must be changing. According to the current model, the Earth is an average of 93 million miles away from the Sun— "average" because the Earth's orbit is slightly elliptical (not exactly circular), so this distance varies a little between summer and winter. This is natural, of course, in the same way that the right and left sides of a person's face are slightly different; but, according to the current model, this average distance is more or less constant.

Although astronomers have not detected this yet, the planets are actually spiraling in toward the Sun, taking billions and billions of years (see Figure 1.1). The spiral is the universal shape

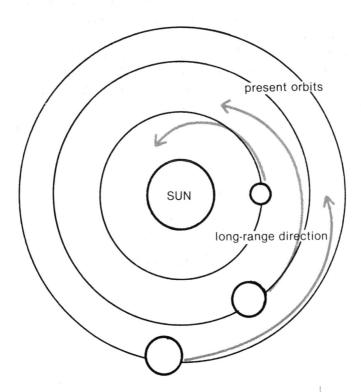

present orbits

SUN

long-range direction

Figure 1.1. All the planets are slowly spiraling in toward the Sun.

or pattern of all phenomena, both large and small. All spirals, including that of our solar system, begin at the outside, or infinite periphery, of space and develop inward until they create a materialized center. Here they change direction, forming a reverse spiral that radiates back out to the periphery.

However, the planets themselves are only the innermost part of this spiral. Beyond the set of orbits is the vast cometary cloud, which consists of about 100 million comets, all with the Sun as their center.

In order to grasp the size of this cometary cloud, let us call the distance from the Sun to the Earth 1 astronomical unit (A.U.). The distance from the Sun to Pluto, the outermost of the nine known planets, is about 40 A.U. So, within a diameter of about 80 A.U., nine planets are orbiting around the Sun. The diameter of the cometary cloud is estimated to be about 3,850 A.U., or about forty-eight to forty-nine times greater than the diameter of Pluto's orbit. In other words, our solar system is actually much larger than we normally think it is.

The structure of the solar system is actually very similar to that of an atom (see Figure 1.2). Again, the present model of atomic structure, developed primarily by the physicist Niels Bohr, overlooks the spiral process of change. The cometary field of the solar system can be compared to an atom's orbiting electrons. Like electrons, comets carry a negative charge. The Sun

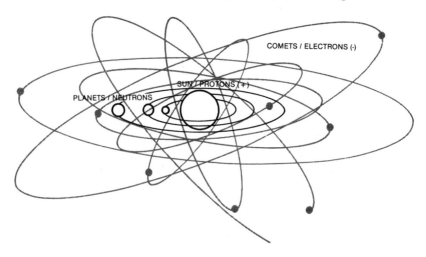

Figure 1.2. "Atomic view" of solar system.

and planets represent the nucleus of the solar system. Like protons in the central part of the atom, the Sun is positively charged. The planets carry a more even balance of charges; they are in effect representing a more neutral charge, something like neutrons.

Comets do not maintain an unchanging orbit. Like planets, they eventually spiral in toward the nucleus. During their long journey, they change form by first taking on, and then eventually discarding, additional mass. A long, long time ago, for example, the planet Pluto was a comet, as were the other planets. A similar process occurs at the subatomic level: electrons eventually spiral in toward the center to become nuclear particles.

Then what is this thing we call the Sun? The prevailing assumption is that the Sun is an independent body composed largely of hydrogen, which changes into helium as it burns away. As the hydrogen continues to burn, the central core of helium grows constantly larger. Scientists believe that this process will eventually exhaust all of the hydrogen in the Sun, and at some point, the Sun will stop burning and die out.

Actually, this way of thinking is similar to the way that sees each part of the body and every disease symptom as arising separately and independently—not seeing that each part of the body originates from the bloodstream that nourishes it. This view is based on isolation rather than integration. It is fragmental and divisive rather than holistic and unifying.

The Sun is not in reality an isolated body burning independently in space. It is simply the central melting point of the entire evolutionary process. Just as comets eventually spiral in to become planets, each planet also spirals in toward the center, gradually losing its satellites and slowly becoming smaller and lighter until it merges with the Sun.

There are currently 107 elements on the Earth. The heaviest of these, such as radium and uranium, are now beginning to evaporate through a process we call radioactivity. They are dissolving, changing from the state of matter to the state of energy. Elements with medium weights, such as calcium and iron, are not presently radioactive; but as the Earth moves closer to the Sun, they will begin to evaporate one by one. Eventually, the planet will exist as a sparkling cloud in which only the very light elements, such as oxygen, nitrogen, and hydrogen, will still exist in their present form.

At the conclusion of this evolutionary process, the light cloud-planet will finally reach that central point, the very center of this huge 3,850-A.U.-wide process known as the solar system, and will instantly radiate out again as highly charged, expanding energy, including the ionized particles of the solar wind. The Sun is the central point where this vast centripetal spiral will turn from its inward course and begin an equally vast centrifugal spiral of radiating energy.

As this stream radiates out in the form of waves and vibrations, it will approach the periphery of the solar system, at which point it will begin to recondense as clouds of gas, eventually forming comets, and again beginning an inward journey toward the center. Over and over, periphery to center and center to periphery, the matter and energy that make up the solar system are constantly recycling.

What are the implications of this holistic model concerning the possibility of life on other planets in the solar system? In my estimate, life first appeared on Earth about 3.2 billion years ago when the planet was in a position somewhere between the present positions of Jupiter and Mars (see Figure 1.3). Early stages of life may well exist at the present time on Mars. In several billion years, Mars will be in our present position in the solar system, and advanced life forms very much like us may well have developed there. Meanwhile, Venus passed through these various positions a long time ago, and life on that planet may have already developed far beyond us.

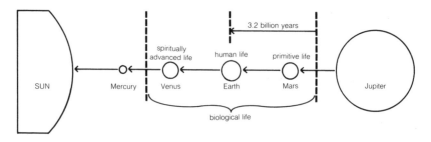

Figure 1.3.   The biological lifespan of the solar system.

Biological life is not an accidental or isolated event. In our solar system, it is part of a continuum that reaches approximately from between Jupiter and Mars to between Venus and Mercury. We can say that this region represents the breeding ground for biological life in our solar system.

According to this new paradigm, human beings may have appeared on Venus millions of years before they appeared on the Earth. It is possible that an advanced civilization capable of interplanetary travel developed on that planet and that visitors from there came to Earth at the time our ancestors were in a primitive state, serving as their teachers, guides, and friends.

Millions of years from now, when the Earth passes beyond the current position of Venus, our planet will begin to dissolve into a vibrational form. At that time, the human beings on Earth will cease to exist in a material form and will instead also evolve into an existence of purely vibrations and waves. Each of us will enter that vibrational world when we die. In that sense, we as individuals will experience the future of the human race as a whole.

UNDISCOVERED PLANETS

Another theory about the origin of UFOs states that they came from a planet that once existed between Mars and Jupiter. The inhabitants of this "fifth planet" developed a high level of civilization and often traveled back and forth between their home planet and the Earth. Contact with the Earth continued until the planet was destroyed, either by a comet or nuclear war. The fragments of this planet were scattered into space, forming what is now the asteroid belt between Mars and Jupiter. Some ancient legends, including those of the Mayans and other American Indian tribes, describe this forgotten planet as the source of extraterrestrial contact.

A related theory, documented at some length by author Zecharia Sitchin in his 1976 book, *The 12th Planet*, is that UFOs are originating from an as-yet-undiscovered planet. Pluto, the farthest known planet from the Sun, is moving at a 14- to 16-degree shift from the solar plane. The undiscovered planet, should it exist, is projected by astronomers to presently be beyond Pluto at a 70-degree angle to the Sun's equator. The presence of a planet in this position would account for inexplicable perturbations in the orbit of Uranus. The discovery of these perturbations around the turn of the century led to the discovery of Pluto in 1930. But early in 1990, Robert Harrington, an astronomer at the United States Naval Observatory, stated that recent analysis has shown that Pluto is 1,000 times too small to be causing the observed perturbations. Harrington has predicted that they are instead being caused by an undiscovered planet—Planet X—presently located in the Southern Hemisphere. Harrington and other researchers are presently searching for Planet X using a telescope in New Zealand.

In his book, Sitchen presents evidence that certain legends, especially those of ancient Sumeria, spoke of this undiscovered planet. These legends state that the planet moves at approximately the same angle that astronomers have been predicting and that its orbit resembles that of a comet. On its closest approach to the Sun, it passes between Mars and Jupiter, and then it begins its journey back to deep space.

Sumerian legends relate that the planet orbits the Sun once every 3,600 years and that it is inhabited by a highly advanced civilization. As the planet approaches the Sun, its inhabitants set out for the Earth in spaceships, then return to their planet as it begins to move back into deep space. Sitchen estimates that the first visitors from this planet may have arrived more than 400,000 years ago and that their landing site is in what is now Saudi Arabia, near to where the Sumerian culture, considered by many to be the birthplace of civilization, emerged.

Modern scientists are puzzled by the wealth of expertise and knowledge utilized by the ancient Sumerians. The Sumerians were the first to develop a system of writing. They invented the wagon wheel and the plow, and had a refined system of measuring and surveying techniques. Their skill in arts and crafts is highly regarded. They divided the day into hours and minutes. Their understanding of astronomy, mathematics, and medicine was vast. Yet despite all these advanced skills and tools, little is known about their origin. Leonard Cattrell, in his book *The Anvil of Civilization*, describes the Sumerian priests this way: "No one knows where they came from; they appear to be related to no race known on earth." According to Sitchen, the Sumerians were aided in their progress by highly intelligent beings from the undiscovered planet.

Sitchen calculates that the undiscovered planet will approach the inner region of the solar system in about another 1,200 years. If this estimate is correct, it would have last approached the Earth about 2,400 years ago, at about the time Ezekiel saw his heavenly vision in the Middle East.

HOW HOT IS THE SUN?

The Isohara maps from Japan include a fascinating drawing showing the region of the Far East connected by a dotted line to a radiating star. The accompanying text states that in ancient times, there was frequent travel back and forth between the two places. The name of the star, according to the maps, is Hitamanokuni, which means "Country of the Sun Globe." (In Japanese, the Earth is referred to as Chikyu, which means "Soil Globe.")

One passage in the text describes an incident in which the emperor of Japan and 397 other people gathered at the top of a high mountain and traveled to the Heavenly Sun Country aboard a flying ship. Certain other cultures around the world also believed that they were descendants of beings from this Heavenly Sun Country and adopted sun symbols on their flags or became known as "sun cultures."

Some interpreters believe that the mysterious radiating star, the "Country of the Sun Globe," is in fact the Sun. But this idea sharply contradicts current thinking about the Sun. According to astronomers, the surface temperature of the Sun is about 6,000°C., and the temperature of the corona, or the extended outer atmosphere, approaches 2,000,000°C. At these temperatures, solid matter instantly vaporizes. However, a small minority of thinkers—including William Herschel, the English astronomer who discovered Uranus—question the assumption that the Sun is hot. Proponents of this latter theory cite as evidence the fact that several comets have been observed entering the huge solar corona and then reappearing unchanged on the opposite side of the Sun. Moreover, they also point out that magnetic activity is supposed to cease under such high temperatures but that the Sun has a strong magnetic field.

According to the theory, the solar corona is something like an aura. The same as the aurora borealis and the human aura that radiates above the head, the corona is composed of very powerful energy, but not in the form of heat. The huge solar aura shoots out streams of ionized particles known as solar wind together with rays of light. As these streams reach the vicinity of Earth, they collide with the atmosphere, and the resulting friction produces the heat. So, although here on the Earth's surface we feel as if the Sun is generating the heat, according to this theory the heat is being created within the Earth's atmosphere itself. If this opinion is correct, the temperatures on Venus and Mercury are not as high as they are currently assumed to be, nor are the temperatures on the outer planets as cold.

I would like to add one additional point from my own view to this theory. The Earth is constantly receiving a force from the heavens that spirals inward toward the core of the planet and then radiates back out as centrifugal force, which we call the Earth's force. This centrifugal force causes the Earth to rotate and stimulates the growth and formation of mountain ranges, plant life, and so-forth. This expanding force also generates heat within the Earth's atmosphere.

As long as a planet is rotating, no matter at what speed, it is throwing off centrifugal force that produces heat. So, according to my estimate, all planets have a reasonable degree of temperature within a range that can support from very primitive up to quite advanced biological life. That would help explain how the undiscovered planet could support human life even though it moves far beyond Pluto in its orbit around the Sun. In other words, we may not be depending exclusively on the Sun for the creation of life; each planet also receives energy directly from outer space and generates its own energy field. All planets may therefore be capable of supporting some form of life.

LIFE IN THE GALAXY

Like the solar system, the Milky Way galaxy is a huge centripetal spiral, with each of its solar systems gradually moving toward its center, taking many hundreds of billions of years. The stars that are close to the galactic center are emitting more yang colors, such as red and infrared, while those that are still further out toward the periphery are emitting more yin colors, such as violet and blue (see Figure 1.4). Our solar system is presently about two-thirds of the way out from the center of the galaxy, so our sun—the center of our cometary-planetary field—is emitting the more balanced, neutral color of yellow.

When seen from the side, the Milky Way resembles a huge flying saucer (see Figure 1.5). It takes this shape because force coming in from the periphery of space pushes toward the center and creates a bulge as it begins to radiate back out. The dimensions of the galaxy are enormous. The Milky Way is about 100,000 light years across and 20,000 light years high. Moreover, astronomers recently discovered a galactic corona, a giant cloud of thin gas surrounding the galaxy and extending outward about 300,000 light years. Estimates place about 100 billion solar systems within the Milky Way.

Given the large number of star systems in the galaxy, there is a high probability that intelligent life exists elsewhere in the

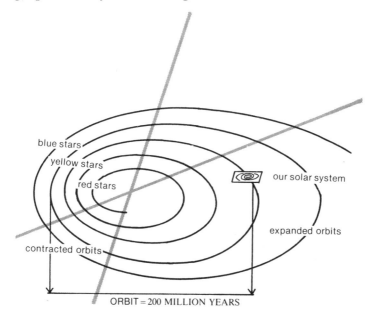

Figure 1.4. The galactic center and the color of stars.

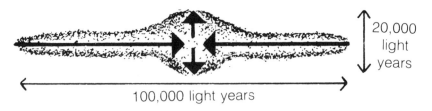

20,000
light
years

100,000 light years

Figure 1.5.   The Milky Way resembles a flying saucer.

Milky Way. If we assume that each of these 100 billion star systems contains at least one planet that is similar to the Earth and has some form of human life, then even if all the other planets in each system do not have any life at all, there are still at least 100 billion planets in our galaxy alone with something resembling human life. If we look beyond our galaxy, we find hundreds of millions of other galaxies, some slightly more developed than ours and some less developed. And each of these galaxies probably contains billions of star systems with planets capable of supporting intelligent life.

We must conclude that there are trillions of other planets in the universe like ours, each with life very much like our own human life. To deny this possibility shows a lack of common sense. Clearly then, there must be life beyond the planet Earth.

However, a number of problems arise when we look toward planets outside our solar system as a possible source of UFOs that visit Earth. One objection to this possibility arises because of the vast distances of interstellar space. The star nearest our solar system, Alpha Centauri, is four light years from our Sun. If a starship were launched from a planet in the Alpha Centauri system, it would have to travel for four years at the speed of light before it reached us. But scientists believe that matter disintegrates at the speed of light, so travel at this speed is considered a physical impossibility. Thus, from a scientific point of view, the possibility of intergalactic travel is far-fetched. If travelers set out from a galaxy a million light years away, they would have to travel at the speed of light for a million years before reaching the Earth.

However, in this universe, energy constantly changes into matter and matter into energy. If human beings could learn how to duplicate this natural process, it might then become possible for them to travel freely across the vastness of interstellar space. In order to do this, people would need to know how to accelerate the vibrational rate of matter and convert it into energy and then how to change it back into matter without losing its original form—in other words, the technology of dematerialization and rematerialization. If a starship could be converted into pure energy, it could conceivably travel faster than the speed of light.

We can project our thoughts instantaneously to far distant places, sending our image millions of light years away. Scientifically speaking, at that time we are using neutrinos, tiny particles that have neither significant mass nor a plus or minus charge. Since they are practically neutral, neutrinos are the medium for intuition, the human faculty of instantaneous insight or awareness. In my estimate, neutrinos travel at the speed of about 100,000 light years per second—or, practically speaking, instantaneously. Streams of these tiny wave-particles are constantly flying back and forth between the planets, stars, and galaxies. If a starship could be converted into a mass of vibrations, it could conceivably ride along one of these streams and travel across incalculable distances at practically instantaneous speeds. Then, once it reached its destination, the starship could be reconverted into solid matter by de-accelerating its vibrational rate.

Another frequently asked question is, Why would civilizations from distant parts of the universe want to investigate the Earth? That question was raised by astronomer Carl Sagan at a 1969 symposium on the UFO phenomenon sponsored by the American Association for the Advancement of Science; the proceedings were published by Cornell University in the 1972 book *UFOs—Scientific Debate*. According to Sagan, the notion that we have been chosen for regular visits by UFOs would mean that we are somehow unique among the civilizations in the universe. That assumption, Sagan declared, "goes against the idea that there are lots of civilizations around. Because if there are lots of them around then the development of our sort of civilization must be pretty common. And if we're not pretty common then there aren't going to be many civilizations advanced enough to send visitors."

This objection centers more around the question of *why* UFOs are visiting the Earth rather than *where* they are coming from or *how* they are getting here. Before we consider that question, however, let us examine one more theory about the origin of UFOs—the idea that they are coming from an entirely different dimension.

PARALLEL WORLDS

Over the centuries, people have often wondered about the existence of parallel worlds or other dimensions. Eastern legends, for example, relate that yogis and other spiritually developed people can project their consciousness into realms that exist beyond the familiar dimensions of time and space. In Japan, these hidden dimensions were given the name *Sen-kyo*, which means "the sphere or realm that can be entered by a person with advanced spiritual powers." According to certain legends, when interdimensional travelers enter that realm, they experience a parallel world very much like our own. That world is inhabited by highly evolved people who can communicate with each other telepathically and travel back and forth between their dimension and ours by flying machine. In addition, certain spiritually developed people in our dimension were also believed to have the ability to communicate telepathically with the people in this other dimension and to summon UFOs from that dimension to ours.

Of course, these beliefs exist beyond the realm of our present science, which can only evaluate things that can be detected by the senses. Could it be, however, that these stories are more than just the product of a fanciful imagination and that parallel dimensions do exist beyond our normal range of perception?

Everything in the universe has a front and a back, or a visible and an invisible side. Our universe came into being not through the "big bang," but through a process that begins when infinity polarizes into *yin* and *yang*, or the energies of expansion and contraction. The energy created by this polarization takes the form of a vast centripetal spiral that condenses into matter, forming galaxies, star systems, planets, plant and animal life, and ultimately man. It is through this process that the large becomes the small, the non-material becomes the material, and the invisible becomes the visible.

That inwardly developing spiral creates the dimension of space that we perceive as our day-to-day reality. However, that spiral does not exist by itself. It coexists with another spiral that forms in the completely opposite direction, moving outward from this tiny, condensed world of matter and back through the world of energy. This centrifugal spiral gives rise to another dimension of space that coexists with ours in the same way that matter exists with antimatter.

Even though we live in both of these dimensions simultaneously, our sensory perception is limited to things that exist within the first, or incoming, spiral. The human nervous system is itself a product of that spiral and is structured so that things enter our range of perception by coming in toward our sense receptors. Our senses are not equipped to deal with an opposite dimension of space that spirals away from us at a very high speed.

As we have seen, our solar system is formed as an inward spiral, the center of which is the Sun. From the Sun, an outgoing spiral arises and moves from the center of the solar system to the periphery. We are unable to see or feel that latter world except vaguely in the form of temperature, light, and radiating energy. That radiating, expanding spiral overlaps the incoming, physical spiral of the solar system. If we consider our centripetal world to be the front, then this centrifugal world is the back that we cannot perceive.

Some people believe that a parallel solar system exists in the invisible realm within this outwardly radiating spiral. They believe this system is close to ours and contains an inhabited planet from which UFOs are periodically launched into our dimension. When UFOs pass through the dimensional barrier, they enter our range of perception and we can see and detect them on radar. But if they accelerate to very high speeds or wavelengths beyond the scope of our radar or the human eye, they pass outside our range of perception. They seem to disappear, and we are left wondering if we ever saw them at all.

WHY ARE THEY COMING?

Through the ages, people have tended to interpret UFOs within the context of their individual world view. Ancient and medieval interpreters therefore adopted a religious or supernatural model to explain UFOs. Ezekiel, for example, referred to his sighting as a "vision of God" and to the sound made by the flying objects as the "voice of the Almighty." In modern times, religious images have been replaced by more scientific ones, since in the modern world, science tends to define the way people look at the world.

A good example of this current model is the theory that when extraterrestrial encounters occurred in the ancient past, the UFO people manipulated the primitive humans they found here and even performed genetic operations in order to create a more intelligent race of slaves. However, this idea is the product of a modern deluded imagination. It mistakenly assigns a modern profit motive to the actions of extraterrestrial visitors and assumes wrongly that their mission was to exploit and compel, rather than to freely assist and guide. I do not believe that visitors from space performed genetic manipulation. Rather, as ancient legends relate, they brought with them knowledge of grain cultivation, natural agriculture, and the way to develop better health, peace, and spiritual consciousness. Through applying what they taught, our ancient ancestors were able to evolve very rapidly. Besides, with a highly developed understanding of the order of the universe, it is unlikely that extraterrestrial visitors would wish to disturb the natural order by employing an artificial and disruptive technique such as genetic engineering.

Many so-called "abduction stories" offer another example of the modern view. For instance, under hypnosis, some people claim to have been abducted by aliens, taken to facilities resembling an operating room, and subjected to often painful and intrusive medical procedures. However, given the current fascination with high-tech medicine, these stories may be more reflections of the "victims'" subconscious fears of medical procedures and the authority of modern medicine than accurate descriptions of the activities of UFO visitors. Moreover, if ancient legends are correct and extraterrestrial visitors are aware of more advanced, natural approaches to healing, it is unlikely that they would employ the highly artificial techniques described in many of these stories.

To some people, extraterrestrial encounters are an extension of the struggles for territory and empire that have occurred throughout history. Like the invading Martians in H. G. Wells's *War of the Worlds,* visitors from space are assumed to be motivated by the desire to conquer humanity and exploit the Earth's natural resources. These misconceptions are the result of trying to view the UFO phenomenon through the narrow prism of recent human experience on Earth. We are simply projecting our fears onto something we do not understand.

Why, then, would extraterrestrial civilizations want to visit the Earth? According to some people, the UFOs recently sighted are paying initial visits from a group of people from many different planets, some within the solar system and some beyond, that calls itself the cosmic federation. Every so often, a civilization in the galaxy reaches a turning point, facing either total destruction or continued evolution. Some civilizations have already solved their problems, passed through the crisis, and gone on to evolve further, while others have not yet reached this stage in their development. Civilizations that did reach the crisis point but failed to pass it may very well have destroyed themselves through a process of biological degeneration or global destruction. The cosmic federation is now visiting here because the Earth is currently facing its time of crisis.

Interestingly, many modern UFO sightings have occurred near facilities that produce or store nuclear weapons, leading some people to speculate that visitors from space are concerned with the spread of nuclear technology or the possibility of nuclear war. Nuclear proliferation has accelerated tremendously since the explosion of the first atomic bomb during World War II. Between 1945 and 1981, for example, six countries developed nuclear weapons and conducted 1,321 atomic explosions both above and below ground. By the early 1980s, forty-eight countries had nuclear reactors or nuclear research reactors that could manufacture weapons-grade material. At present, there is no safe storage method for nuclear waste. Plutonium-239 has a half-life of 240,000 years and uranium-238 has a half-life of 4.5 million years, posing a lethal threat not only to future generations on Earth, but also to the balanced ecology of the solar system as a whole.

Moreover, the United States and Soviet Union together possess an estimated 40,000 to 50,000 nuclear weapons totaling 15,000 megatons of destructive capability; the Hiroshima bomb had a strength of .03 megaton. About 15,000 of these warheads are poised for land- or sea-based missile delivery. Modern nuclear submarines each carry up to eight times the total firepower that was available during World War II, and a single missile can be launched containing ten warheads that are each independently targeted to destroy a different city. If a world-scale nuclear war broke out, it would not only totally destroy humanity, but it might also fragment the planet and send pieces of radioactive rock hurtling into space. In that case, our relation with the Moon and our neighboring planets of Venus and Mars, along with all our other so-called "gravitational" or energetic relationships, would drastically change, throwing the entire solar system into confusion and scattering radioactive waste throughout the galaxy. Even without a full-scale nuclear war, the continued destruction of our environment—including the cutting down of tropical rain forests and the pollution of the air, water, and soil—could trigger massive climactic and geological changes, altering the Earth's rotation and disrupting its relationship with the other bodies in the solar system.

Throughout history, there have been many prophecies of such catastrophic events. These things were foreseen by prophets such as Edgar Cayce, Jesus in the Book of Revelations, the prophet Isaiah in the Old Testament, Nostradamus, and many other seers. These things are also vividly foretold in the various cannons and sutras of Buddhism.

Of the thousands of sutras, or teachings, in Buddhism, two deal specifically with the end of the world. One, the "Sutra of the Miroku Bodhisattva Descending," tells of Miroku Bodhisattva, the so-called Buddha of the Future, who will save the planet. According to this sutra, the Miroku Bodhisattva has been teaching day and night to thousands of followers at some place in the heavens, but at the time of the end of the world, he will come down to save many people and establish spiritual consciousness throughout the world. The sutra then very vividly describes the end of the world and this salvation.

The other sutra is the "Sutra of the Time of the Perishing of Buddha's Teachings." According to this sutra, all of Buddha's teachings will be forgotten some time in the future, and at that time, mankind and the Earth will face a great catastrophe. Again there is a vivid description of the great misery and suffering, followed by a depiction of how a new world of health, peace, and spiritual understanding will arise.

These prophecies could be interpreted to mean that humanity will gain a true understanding of the order of the universe and will learn how to live in peace, health, and harmony on the Earth. Or they could mean that the cosmic federation, or some other spiritually advanced beings from another planet or dimension, will come to help save the Earth at the critical time. However, if UFOs are in fact planning to save the Earth, we might ask—as one American scientist once did—about UFOs and extraterrestrial visitors, "Why should one not have landed and shown himself to the President of the United States, to a member of the National Academy of Sciences, or at least to some member of Congress?" It seems that in recent times at least, extraterrestrial visitors have been following a policy of nonintervention in earthly affairs. Perhaps they feel that we must learn how to pass through this critical time by ourselves.

We on Earth created the present crisis, and it is therefore up to us to solve it. As practitioners of natural healing know very well, a sick person must take the responsibility for his condition and change his diet, lifestyle, and way of thinking in order to recover completely and avoid further illness. Other people can offer guidance or advice, but it is the patient himself who must make the necessary changes. Similarly, we as a species must change our self-destructive patterns and prevent these global catastrophes from ever occurring. The best way to do this is by ourselves, without the intervention of anyone else. If we are unable to change our direction and prevent global destruction by ourselves, then there is a good chance that beings from another world will intervene, not necessarily with the intention to save us, but rather to preserve the solar system.

Even though they have not yet intervened directly, extraterrestrial visitors may have already begun to offer a very quiet and subtle form of assistance by helping us to reawaken our common sense. The search for extraterrestrials has stimulated us to recall our ancient past, including the tradition of eating whole cereal grains, which they may have established a long time ago on Earth as the biological foundation for health and peace. And they may well have offered us a glimpse of the future by encouraging us to unite as one humanity in order to overcome our difficulties and evolve toward the stars.

This remarkable photograph was taken on March 8, 1975 in Ober-Sadelegg, Switzerland. Looking across an open field, the cameraman spied a UFO slowly moving toward the distant tree line some 650 feet away. He calculated the circular object to be approximately 20 feet in diameter.

2.

Energy Medicine

> ... These our actors,
> As I foretold you, were all spirits, and
> Are melted into air, into thin air:
> And, like the baseless fabric of this vision,
> The cloud-capp'd towers, the gorgeous palaces,
> The solemn temples, the great globe itself,
> Yea, all which it inherit, shall dissolve
> And, like this insubstantial pageant faded,
> Leave not a rack behind. We are such stuff
> As dreams are made on; and our little life
> Is rounded with a sleep. ...
>
> Shakespeare
> *The Tempest*

Our bodies are composed of trillions and trillions of atoms. To our senses, the body appears to be composed of solids, liquids, and gases. But in reality, the body is nothing but a mass of energy and vibrations. All of our cells, tissues, bones, and organs are made up of energy and are constantly changing.

Thousands of years ago, Oriental cultures understood this. They used the term *ki* to describe the universal energy that makes up all things, including the human body, and they developed comprehensive systems of healing based on this understanding. The word "ki" is still used in Asian countries to describe everyday things and occurrences. Sickness, for example, is called *byo-ki* in Japanese. We can interpret it to mean that someone's energy or ki has become chaotic or out of order. Mental illness is referred to as *ki-chigai*, or "wrong ki." It is also called *kyo-ki*. Interestingly, the Chinese character for "kyo" means literally "beast." The Japanese word for personality is *ki-sho*, which means the "nature" or "character" of someone's ki. Weather is called *ten-ki,* or literally the "ki of heaven." Similarly, a very dim, dark, and depressive character or place is said to have *yin-ki,* while a happy, bright, and active character or place has *yo-ki. Yo* is the Japanese word for the Chinese word *yang.*

HEAVEN AND EARTH

Ancient people understood that ki is governed by two universal forces: one coming in upon the Earth and the other going out from the Earth toward space. The incoming force, which is moving from the infinite periphery of space toward the center of the Earth, they called *heaven.* And the outgoing force, which is moving from the center of the Earth toward the periphery of space, they called *Earth.* The force of Earth is generated by the rotation of the planet on its axis.

Heaven's force moves in a centripetal, or inward, direction and causes contraction. Ancient people classified it as yang. They also noticed that Earth's force moves in a centrifugal, or expanding, direction and classified it as yin. Both forces move toward the surface of the Earth, one from external space and the other from the center of the Earth. And both forces appear in the structure and function of all things on the planet.

The Earth discharges the most centrifugal force along the equator, where the movement of rotation has its greatest power. Heaven's force is strongest at the poles, especially at the North Pole. These are the most intense regions of charge, but every area of the planet is charged to some degree by both forces.

All things on Earth, including air, water, and soil, are created and governed by the combined forces of heaven and Earth. Moreover, all things on the planet are composed of these two opposite-yet-complementary tendencies. In other words, all things have both the tendency of contraction and the tendency of expansion within them. In the same way, whatever appears on the Earth—whether it be plant or animal life, the motion of ocean currents or clouds, or the development of civilizations and cultures—is governed by these two forces: heaven, which is yang, and Earth, which is yin.

This way of thinking is not at all contradictory to ancient thinking in the West. The Bible says that in the beginning, God created heaven and Earth, and between them, all things came into being. This is exactly the same as the traditional philosophy of the East. "Heaven" means, as far as the Earth is concerned, all celestial influence coming in upon the planet. "Earth" means all of the expanding influence that is being exerted up from the center of the Earth and is moving outward to the infinite periphery of space.

In plants, Earth's force influences more the growth and structure of the leaves and flowers, while heaven's force has a greater influence on the roots. The human body is created by the same forces. The head develops upward and is influenced by Earth's force, while the rest of the body develops in a downward direction under the influence of heaven. At present, heaven's downward force is in general about seven times stronger than Earth's rising energy. The range of strength of Earth's force to heaven's force is about one-to-five to one-to-ten.

Earth's upward force causes our head hair to grow. It also causes the female sexual organs to develop upward. It flows up through a woman's body and charges the tongue, so her tongue is very moveable. Her hair also grows longer, and she often wears high-heeled shoes. Men receive a stronger charge of heaven's force and so wear lower heels; have deeper, lower voices; and have facial and body hair that grows downward. Heaven's force also creates the uvula at the back of the throat, and in men causes another big uvula (the penis) to appear in the lower body.

Heaven and Earth are the sources of energy for all our bodily functions. They are especially active along a central line that runs deep within the body. Heaven's and Earth's forces collide along this line and produce highly charged centers of energy known as *chakras*. There are seven of these highly charged centers in the body located along the central line (see Figure 2.1). The collision of heaven's and Earth's forces in the chakras creates spirals of energy. Energy also comes in and goes out through the hands and feet, charging the limbs with life force.

Heaven's force enters the body through the spiral chakra at the top of the head. It flows downward and charges the midbrain chakra and all of the cerebral cells. Each brain cell is like a

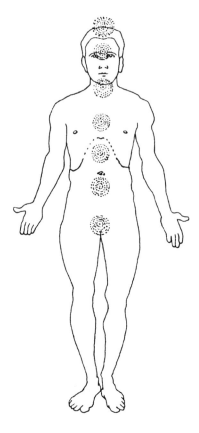

Figure 2.1.   The location of the seven chakras.

television set, receiving vibrations and translating them into certain wavelengths to create thoughts and images. The brain would not function without the energy supplied by the mid-brain chakra and the spiral chakra on the top of the head.

Similarly, without the energy provided by the throat chakra, the thyroid and parathyroid glands would not secrete any hormones, nor would the vocal cords be capable of speech. In the chest, the heart and lungs expand and contract because of the energy supplied by the heart chakra, while the secretion of pancreatic hormones and gastric acids results from the activity of the stomach chakra. In the small intestine, the hara chakra enables the intestines to digest and absorb food. This chakra is known in Oriental countries as *ki-kai,* or "ocean of energy," and it is here that implantation of the fertilized ovum takes place. New human life develops here because of the intense charge of heaven's and Earth's forces in this region. Finally, the energy generated in the seventh and lowest chakra—which is the entrance point for Earth's force and the exit point for heaven's force—creates sexual desire. In men, this chakra is charged by heaven's force, and in women, by Earth's force. These oppositely charged poles attract and unite during sex.

The body's energy system is related to the energy systems of other things in nature, including the Earth. From the North Pole and also from the South Pole, ki comes into the Earth in the form of a centripetal spiral. Its function is to condense or contract, and it forms the Earth's core, mantle, and crust. A similar process takes place in fruits, vegetables, and the human body. Using an apple as an example may make this easier to understand.

The apple's core, or central area where the seeds are produced, corresponds to the core of the Earth. The pulp is equivalent to the Earth's mantle, and the skin, to the crust and surface of the Earth. In the body, the chakras and the main channel of energy are equivalent to the Earth's core, while the organs, tissues, and internal structures correspond to the mantle. The skin is equivalent to the crust and surface. The places where heaven's and Earth's forces enter and leave the body—the spiral chakra on the top of the head and the sexual chakra in the lower body—correspond to the Earth's North and South Poles.

The aurora borealis, or "northern lights," radiates light and energy above the North Pole. The aurora australis radiates light and energy above the South Pole. Scientists believe that these brilliant lights are created when high energy particles coming from the Sun collide with atoms and molecules in the upper atmosphere. These energetic particles (mainly electrons and protons) are constantly discharged from the Sun as a part of the "solar wind." When they arrive in the vicinity of the Earth, they are caught in the downward spiral of heaven's force at the poles. Similarly, above each person's head is an energy field known as the *aura*. To the specially trained eye, the human aura radiates a variety of colors that correspond to a person's health and mental state. A healthy aura has a golden-white color. If the aura has a darker shade, it is often an indication of physical or mental imbalance.

We can carry this comparison even further. Electromagnetic lines or belts radiate outward from the Earth's core in a north-south direction. Similar lines are found in pumpkins, squash, onions, watermelons, and other fruits and vegetables. These highly charged lines cause the Earth's crust to bulge outward, and mountain ranges are formed as a result. The undersea mid-Atlantic and mid-Pacific ridges are parts of this energy system, as are the Rockies, Andes, Himalayas, and other mountains on the surface of the Earth. Many of the Earth's mountains, including those under the oceans, are volcanically active. Strong currents of energy from the North and South Poles gather toward the center of the Earth, creating high temperatures and active motion that cause the elements at the core to become semi-liquid or molten. These forces charge the core and radiate outward toward the mountain ranges at the surface. At certain points along the mountain ranges, eruptions of energy—in the form of volcanoes—arise.

An interesting thing happens to the Earth after it rotates on its axis for thousands of years: the axis shifts, causing a change in the Earth's rotation. An axis shift occurs in a matter of days and is similar to what happens when a spinning top suddenly flips on its side and begins rotating in a different direction. The Earth's axis has shifted many times in the past, and as a result, some mountains run east-west, others run north-south, and still others run in directions that are in-between.

Ancient people were well aware of the Earth's invisible energy system. Because the mountains are strongly charged with Earth's force, people would often go into the Himilayas, the Andes, or mountains in China and Japan to practice meditation and other forms of spiritual training. In Japan, people who went to the mountains to develop spiritual abilities were known as *Sen-Nin*. Sen-Nin were rarely seen by ordinary people, and according to legend, they had all kinds of extraordinary powers, such as the ability to fly, change common elements into gold, and live for several hundred years. These abilities are similar to those that were attributed to certain yogis who lived in the Himilayas.

Future Energy Sources

Modern energy sources are often wasteful and inefficient. They deplete the Earth's natural resources and pollute the environment. Modern people are unfortunately unaware of the real nature of energy, and therefore cannot find ways to use it that do not eventually create problems bigger than those they solve. Ancient people, on the other hand, understood this very well and were able to create wonderful, effective, non-polluting technologies.

Below are two ideas for tapping into unlimited sources of energy based on an understanding of the flow of heaven's and Earth's forces and of the endless currents of ki found throughout the universe.

1. *The Geological Method. While the Earth rotates, throwing off energy from the equator, tremendous streams of celestial energy are also coming in through the poles. These streams are coursing through the entire planet, forming huge lines of electromagnetic energy; along these highly charged energy belts, mountain ranges are being formed, running from north to south. (Some mountain ranges run east to west. These were formed prior to the recent shifts of the Earth's axis and show the outline of the Earth's previous north-south orientation.)*

   As we know from acupuncture and Oriental medicine, the energy in the body's meridians surfaces at various points (these points are actually more like tiny holes). These points are used to adjust the body's energy, either pouring in more energy if a deficiency exists or draining off energy if the point is excessively charged.

   These points correspond to the Earth's volcanoes, such as Mount St. Helens and Mount Vesuvius. If we can develop a method to channel into these points, as we do in acupuncture with a fine needle, energy could be drawn off and distributed to the entire world. As long as the Earth is rotating and the cosmos exist, this energy source is unlimited.

2. *The Solar Wind Method. Within the continuous stream of energy radiating from the Sun to the Earth are many preatomic particles, including ionized protons and electrons. As this current approaches the Earth, it separates: the more-yang particles, such as the positively charged protons, are attracted to the more-yin evening side of the Earth, while the more-yin, negatively charged electrons are attracted to the more-yang morning side of the Earth. At the side of the Earth facing directly away from the Sun, high above the atmosphere at about 2 a.m., these polarized streams of plus- and minus-charged energetic particles collide with a tremendous force. If we are awake at this time, we can sense this energy and are often very easily inspired or spiritually charged.*

   As long as the Sun is radiating toward the Earth, this powerful collision and energy-generation takes place. If we could shoot a satellite up to the place of collision, we could send down to the Earth's surface a continuous stream of vast, unlimited energy.

   To create a practical way for implementing either of these two methods, only minor technical problems need to first be solved. Either method alone could easily fulfill the world's total energy needs. Then what would become of the nuclear energy controversy? Or of the power struggle for control of the world's petroleum reserves?

The body also has a system of highly charged energy lines. As we have already seen, energy enters the body through its north and south poles, creating and charging the chakras, organs, and bodily functions. It radiates out from the center of the body the same way it radiates outward from the core of the Earth. These radiating lines in the body are also highly charged with energy and are called *meridians*. Numerous points that carry a more intense charge of energy arise along the meridians. Energy from the environment streams into the body through these points, and energy from inside the body flows out through them. These highly charged places are like volcanoes and are known as *meridian points*. They are used in acupuncture, shiatsu, and other traditional methods of healing to rebalance the body's energy system.

We can also compare the body's energy system to the structure of a plant. Plants are rooted in the soil, and Earth's force causes them to branch upward above the ground. Our roots are in heaven: we receive cosmic energy through the spiral chakra on the top of the head. Each hair also conducts heaven's force. In plants, energy flows upward from the roots, while in the human body, energy flows downward from the head, charging and nourishing the central channel, chakras, organs, limbs, and other parts of the body. Plants are yin and expanded, so energy spirals outward from the stem, forming branches and leaves. The human body is compacted; energy spirals inward from the meridians, forming cells and tissues. From the chakra line, it branches into fourteen main streams or meridians, which run just below the surface of the skin. Each meridian then subdivides into millions and even trillions of smaller branches that ultimately connect with each of the body's cells.

A plant's leaves open toward the outside, while the cells of the body develop internally. Energy from heaven, from the whole universe, as well as from the Earth, constantly charges each cell with life force. Cells also receive a constant supply of materialized energy in the form of oxygen and nutrients supplied by the bloodstream. Our life and health depend on the harmonious balance between these two currents of energy: the current streaming in from the environment and the one being generated internally through the metabolism of food.

Similarly, branching off from the Earth's mountain ranges, or meridians, are invisible lines of energy that form a sort of power grid on the planet's surface. Ancient people tracked these invisible energy pathways and often cleared the land above them. These manmade tracks, called *ley lines* (from the Saxon word for "meadow" or "cleared strip of land"), correspond to the streams of energy that branch off from the body's meridians. They also link megalithic structures such as Stonehenge and have been found throughout the British Isles, Europe, and the Andes. In western Bolivia, these lines are called *ta-kis*, which according to the local Indians means "spirit paths." Interestingly, the word "ki" was used by the ancient Andeans to describe energy or spirit just as it was by the Japanese.

Ancient people often built stone circles, temples, and burial mounds on spots where two or more of these lines intersected. In the 1970s, a British writer-explorer used infrared photography to find numerous such straight lines radiating out from the Inca Temple of the Sun, in Cuzco, Peru. Later people built churches on many of these old sites; many medieval churches in Germany, England, Ireland, and throughout Europe stand on these lines, as do early Spanish colonial churches in Central and South America. Ancient people were sensitive to the strong charge of Earth's force in these places and, as they did with the charge in the mountains, considered it to be helpful for spiritual development.

MICROCOSM EQUALS MACROCOSM

The present scientific view of the human body is largely anatomical and mechanistic. It was arrived at by dividing dead tissue into parts and calling each part a different name, such as "lung," "liver," or "blood cell." We ourselves are accustomed to thinking in this way, so we usually refer to our external features as distinct, autonomous entities, such as "my hair," "my arm," "my nose," and so on. However, this fragmented way of looking at existence misses the point about the real nature and meaning of the living human body.

When we look at a real, living human being, the first thing we notice is that he is living within a huge environment and constantly exchanging energies with that environment. Of course, a person cannot live without a heart, liver, or blood. If these vital organs are removed, he dies, and his identity as a human being disappears. But suppose we took away the Sun, removed the atmosphere, or took away the galaxies in the sky—what would happen? Again, he could not live. So which is really the body: that assemblage of internal features or that array of external features? Which one is really a person's identity?

Actually, both are. The small human shape and the huge natural environment are both formed according to the same principles. If you examine a human hair under a microscope, you will be surprised to see how closely it resembles a tree. Both are created in the form of a spiral. The main constituent of a tree is related to carbohydrates, while that of human hair is keratin, a form of protein. These organic compounds are complementary and antagonistic. But the shape and process of growth of both these structures are very nearly identical, differing only in scale or size.

The same as the growth of plants, hair growth changes with the seasons. During the summer, we tend to take in more yin factors in our diet in order to balance with the warmer temperatures. From the nutrients we take in, we use a smaller percentage for active metabolism and generation of body heat. One of the ways we balance this out is to eat less. Another way is to discharge some of the excess in the form of hair. Moreover, in the atmosphere, Earth's yin or rising energy becomes stronger during the spring and summer. The increase in yin, upward energy stimulates the growth of head hair and, in nature, causes plants to become more lush and expanded.

Conversely, in the autumn and winter, heaven's contracting energy becomes stronger. This slows the rate of hair growth and causes plants to become more sparse, contracted, and dormant. During the winter, we tend to increase the intake of contracting factors in our diet to balance with the cold, and more of what we take in is used for active metabolism and the generation of body heat. We then balance this by eating a little more and by holding more of what we take in inside the body rather than discharging it in the form of head hair.

Just as the roots of plants are enclosed by soil, the root of each hair is enclosed by a hair follicle. Growing and multiplying cells are found in the bulb of the hair root. Blood capillaries in the papilla provide nourishment to the hair through the root. Just as plants depend on the quality of the nutrients in the soil, hair depends on the quality of the nutrients supplied by the bloodstream. What we eat and drink is crucial in determining the health and appearance of our hair.

As we saw earlier, the many volcanoes located around the planet correspond to the nearly 400 acupuncture points, or *tsubo*, located along the body's energy meridians. Actually, the more correct translation of "tsubo" is not "point," but "hole." A tsubo is actually a hole through which ki energy enters and exits the body. Each tsubo is constantly discharging energy the same way a volcano discharges lava. Running beneath the Earth's surface are great currents of magma, the thickly condensed, highly charged streams of molten rock that nourish volcanoes. These currents correspond to our own meridians of acupuncture, or channels of ki flow, which run just below the body's surface.

The salty oceans, as you can well imagine, are replicated in our bloodstream. When life first emerged from the primordial ocean, the salty sea was internalized in the bloodstream. Blood is a replica of the ancient ocean in which early life evolved. The clear liquid—or lymph fluid—that appears when we cut ourselves corresponds to the Earth's reservoirs of fresh water. Our lymph streams run throughout our body, eventually connecting with our more centralized bloodstream. In the same way, streams of fresh water run throughout the Earth, eventually connecting with the more centralized sea.

What about the air? The air we also take inside ourselves and carry throughout the body to nourish all our cells. Then what about the trillions of stars in the sky? They correspond to the trillions of cells in the body.

When life first began on this planet roughly 3.2 billion years ago, its structure consisted of only a single cell. At that time, the Earth's atmosphere was thick and dense, so only one star, the Sun, was close and bright enough to penetrate to the planet's surface and influence the formation of cells. Then, as the atmosphere gradually cleared, the radiation from other stars, planets, and celestial bodies started to penetrate, creating and correlating to more and more individual cells, until life eventually took the form of very complex, multi-cellular organisms.

In the night sky, we can detect many huge star clusters, or galaxies. Galaxies correspond to our various organs, glands, muscles, and other large groupings of cells. Between these galaxies and groups of galaxies are coursing very high-speed currents of electromagnetic energy, corresponding to the currents of nervous impulses and ki flow that connect all the parts of the body.

Our small human bodies are actually very condensed replicas of our environment, embracing within them all the factors that make up the huge external universe. Inside equals outside, large equals small, and small equals large. When we talk about man, or when we consider the future of humanity, we are actually talking about the future of the universe itself. There is no distinction, no separation, between human beings and their environment, both near and far.

ORGAN STRUCTURE

Everything on the planet is created by both heaven's force and Earth's force, or—we can say—by yin and yang. There is nothing that is made by heaven's force alone; such a thing would become smaller and smaller, contracting to the point of infinite smallness. And there can be nothing that is made exclusively by Earth's force. If there was this type of thing, it would become bigger and bigger until it merged with infinity itself.

So, because something exists, we know that heaven's force and Earth's force are both present. But the proportion of these forces varies in each thing. Some things have more Earth's force and other things have more heaven's force. The difference between things is a matter of the degree to which these two forces exist. The fact that no two things have the exact same proportion of heaven's and Earth's forces makes life very interesting. Because of that, no two things are identical, and everything is different from everything else.

Of course, similar things exist in nature. Human beings appear very similar to one another when compared with cows or crocodiles, yet among the billions of humans on the planet, no two are exactly alike. Before even looking at them, we know that their birthdates are different, their birth times are different, their chewing manners are different, their activities are different, and so on. But even though no two people are the same, everyone is made up of a combination of the two primary energies. And the differences between us are due only to the differing proportions of these two universal tendencies. Now, let us apply these principles to see how heaven and Earth influence the internal organs and the structure of the body as a whole.

The lungs are not made by either heaven's force or Earth's force alone. But even though both these forces are there, only one is dominant. Within the lungs, which of these forces is stronger? Earth's force is more active in the upper regions of the body and is the predominant force influencing the lungs. Earth's force enters the body through the feet and the sexual chakra and gathers in the center of the abdomen. From there, it travels up along the primary channel. Of course, it doesn't move in a straight line. The Earth is rotating, so Earth's force moves in an ascending spiral.

In order to understand this better, we can look at the large intestine, which is opposite and complementary to the lungs. The lungs are located in the upper body, and absorb and release gas (more yin), while the large intestine is located in the lower body and deals with liquids and solids (more yang). The lungs are a pair of very dense organs, but the large intestine, in opposition, is one very long organ. Which of the forces is stronger in the large intestine? Heaven's force is more active in the lower body and in the large intestine. But although heaven's force is stronger, Earth's force is still coming in, so the large intestine does not go straight down.

Earth's force causes the large intestine to go upward on the right side of the body. In the body's middle region, the large intestine goes straight across, curving slightly down, and on the left side, it goes down. On the whole, the large intestine has a going-down tendency, but it cannot go straight down because of Earth's force, which is going up. According to this, on which side of the body—right or left—is Earth's force predominant?

Earth's upward energy is more active on the right side of the body, while heaven's force is stronger on the left.

Now let's compare the large intestine to the small intestine. The small intestine also moves downward. So again, heaven's force is predominant. But why does the small intestine wind back and forth rather than going straight down? Again, because the force of the Earth is resisting, pushing up. But since heaven's force is stronger, the small intestine eventually does go down.

The liver has more of a yang structure. It is tight and solid. Therefore, it is constructed in the form of a centripetal spiral. Conversely, the gall bladder is more hollow. It is made by a centrifugal spiral moving from the center to the periphery. The liver and gall bladder are opposite in structure yet function as a unit. On the whole, Earth's force is stronger in this organ-pair, although when the body is divided into the lower, middle, and upper regions, the lowest region is charged by heaven's force, the middle region is balanced between the two energies, and the uppermost region is dominated by Earth's force. But since the right side is strongly influenced by Earth's force, the liver and gall bladder are charged primarily by upward energy.

The spleen and pancreas are located on the opposite side of the body, where we also have a large empty organ, the stomach. The spleen and pancreas are more yang, contracted organs and are created in the form of a centripetal spiral. The stomach is open and hollow, and is created in the form of a centrifugal spiral. On the whole, these organs are influenced by the downward flow of heaven's force on the left side of the body.

The heart is located in the center of the chest along the main chakra line. Its four chambers are each different, yet function as one unit. The chambers on the right side of the heart take in or gather blood from the body and send it out to the lungs; those on the left send blood out to the body after it comes in from the lungs. In addition, the heart also receives a strong charge of heaven's and Earth's forces directly from the primary energy channel, which it distributes through the blood to trillions of cells in the body.

Although the heart is one unit, each side functions differently. The right side functions in a more yang way, gathering blood from the periphery in toward the center. But this part of

the heart must become more yin—structurally more expanded—in order to do this. The right atrium is therefore larger
than the left and is strongly charged by Earth's force. The left
side functions in a yin way—sending blood outward from the
heart to the body—yet its structure is more yang or compacted.
Of the sections of the heart, the left ventricle has the thickest,
most muscular wall. Its strong power of contraction is made
possible by the charge of heaven's force on the left side of the
body.

Heaven's and Earth's forces work together in the heart, but
which of the two is stronger? Earth's force predominates
slightly, and so the heart is located in the upper region of the
body.

As we have seen, Earth's force flows up the right side of the
body and heaven's force flows down the left side. So naturally,
the left and right kidneys must be a little different from each
other. How does this manifest? The size, position, and function
of each kidney differ slightly from those of the other. The right
kidney is more expanded and located a little higher up, while
the left kidney is more contracted and lower down in the body.
So, the left kidney is a little more yang and the right kidney is a
little more yin. The size and shape of each kidney's cells, and
also the function of each kidney, differ slightly.

No two things in this universe are identical. This is true for the
left and right ovaries, testicles, nostrils, feet, eyes, and other
paired structures in the body. You can see this every day by looking at the people you meet. Perfect symmetry doesn't exist in nature. It is an artificial concept that exists only in the human mind.

Each of the body's organs is a manifestation of energy, and
each is unique. In Table 2.1, we categorize the major organs accord-

Table 2.1. Body Organs and Influential Force

Heaven's Force	Earth's Force
Large intestine	Lungs
Small intestine	Liver
Spleen, pancreas, stomach	Gall bladder
Left side of heart	Right side of heart
Left kidney	Right kidney

ing to which force has the strongest influence on them. Understanding the body as energy is but one part of the ancient understanding of ki. Yet it gave rise to a comprehensive system of healing based on a profound understanding of humanity and nature.

HEALING WITH ENERGY

Food is a condensed form of energy. It represents the crystallization of sunlight, air, water, and soil, and provides the substance out of which we create our physical bodies. The quality of our food determines the quality of our blood, cells, and tissues, and hence the overall condition of our health.

Some foods accelerate heaven's force and others accelerate Earth's force. Let's take ginger root as an example. Which force does ginger root accelerate in the body? Ginger has a strong, spicy flavor and an expanding tendency. It accelerates the charge of Earth's force and causes blood and energy to flow outward toward the surface of the body. On the other hand, meat is very condensed. It accelerates heaven's force, as does salt, which is another strongly contractive substance. In general, plant foods accelerate expanding force, while animal foods activate descending and contracting energy.

Sugar, chocolate, oil, fruit, and fruit juice are all strongly expansive and accelerate the flow of Earth's force. Whole grains are generally balanced, although Earth's force predominates slightly because they are plants. However, the influence of heaven's force can be seen in the compact structure of grains. Soft drinks, such as diet soda and cola beverages, are strongly expansive and accelerate Earth's force. Foods that are cooked for a long time are more condensed and accelerate heaven's force, while salads and quick, lightly cooked dishes activate Earth's energy. Microwave radiation is extremely expansive and causes foods to "cook" very rapidly; microwave ovens are not recommended for optimal health. Eggs are very condensed and activate heaven's force, while coffee stimulates the more yin front portions of the brain and activates Earth's force.

A healthful diet is one that avoids extremes of either energy and is based on a moderate balance of heaven's and Earth's forces. In a temperate, four-season climate, this means a diet based on balanced whole grains, beans, local vegetables, sea vegetables, and supplementary foods such as low-fat white-meat fish, local fruits, seeds, and non-caffeine teas. This dietary pattern is referred to as the standard macrobiotic diet. However, balancing heaven's and Earth's forces in our diet does not mean balancing them fifty-fifty but rather dynamically according to our condition and circumstances.

If we are successful at striking a balance between heaven and Earth, then the functioning and quality of all our organs and body as a whole are generally assured. A naturally balanced diet is therefore essential for remaining free of sickness. But if we take in foods that cause Earth's force to become too active, or that over-stimulate heaven's force, then the functions of certain organs may be accelerated while those of others are reduced. No one food or medicine is good for the entire body. If it is beneficial for one part, it is usually inhibiting for another part. Something that stimulates the liver may also inhibit the spleen, while a food that strengthens the heart could weaken the kidneys. This is why traditional herbal medicines contain a balanced combination of yin and yang ingredients and why a naturally balanced diet includes a wide variety of foods with complementary energies.

This principle also applies to modern medicines, such as aspirin and antibiotics. Aspirin, for example, is strongly charged with Earth's expanding force. Being expansive, it thins the blood and slows the rate at which cholesterol and fat accumulate in the arteries. However, it can also cause blood vessels to expand and erupt, resulting in bleeding. Someone with a weak or dilated circulatory system could hemorrhage from taking too much aspirin. Similarly, antibiotics diminish the symptoms of infection, but at the same time weaken the body's natural immunity and remove beneficial microorganisms from the intestines. In general, the stronger and more effective a medicine is for eliminating a specific symptom, the more potential it has to disrupt the functioning of the body as a whole.

Sickness arises when the body's energy system becomes imbalanced or extreme. Cancer, heart disease, arthritis, and other sicknesses arise because energy is out of balance. Problems such as too much upward or downward energy, overactive or stagnant energy, and too much or not enough energy in certain parts of the body can all produce sickness.

Traditionally, Oriental medicine approached sickness from the point of view of energy. Oriental healing methods were aimed at correcting imbalances—supplying energy when it is weak or reducing it when it is excessive. Illnesses were generally classified into two categories. Those resulting from underactive or deficient energy were referred to by the ancient Chinese as *kyo-tsu*, which means "empty symptom." Sicknesses that result from overactive or excessive energy were referred to as *ji-tsu*, which means literally "full symptom." Today, Oriental doctors often refer to these as simply *kyo* and *jitsu*.

Conditions such as malnutrition and low blood pressure caused by a weak heart are examples of deficient energy and would be considered kyo, while symptoms such as high fever, frequent coughing, excessive sweating, and obesity are a result of overactive energy and would be classified as jitsu. Foods, herbal medicines, and other treatments were used to correct these imbalances. Some treatments were used because they activate and supply energy, and other treatments were used for their calming and tranquilizing effects. A variety of grains, vegetables, beans, sea vegetables and other plant foods, herbs, and in some cases minerals and animal foods were employed for these purposes.

These principles were applied not only to the use of foods and herbal medicines, but also to techniques such as shiatsu, acupuncture, and palm healing. Acupuncture, for example, can be used to either activate or calm the body's energy flow. If the needle is left in for a long period, it acts like a television antenna, picking up energy from the atmosphere and channeling it through the point and meridian to deep within the body, thereby activating the corresponding organ. But if the needle is put in for only a short time and withdrawn with a slight clockwise motion, it has the effect of drawing energy out of the body and sedating the meridian and organ.

Moxabustion, or burning dried mugwort (moxa) on an acupuncture point, is an energy-supplying, activating treatment. This technique has been used for thousands of years in China and Japan. Moxa is very good for helping underactive conditions, such as chronic constipation caused by a lack of peristalsis in the intestine and fatigue or exhaustion in the kidneys resulting from over-intake of fluid. However, because it supplies energy, moxabustion is not good for inflammations and fevers, which arise when energy becomes overactive.

External compresses were also used frequently as a part of the traditional practice of energy medicine and are used today as a part of macrobiotic home care. Certain compresses activate and supply energy, while others calm and reduce it. A ginger compress is made by dipping towels into hot water in which ginger root has been dissolved. The hot ginger towels are then applied repeatedly to the needy part of the body until the skin becomes red. A ginger compress is generally an energy-activating or energy-supplying treatment. Its opposite is a cold or cool compress, such as one made with mashed tofu or green vegetables, which diminishes or sedates overactive energy. If someone is experiencing intestinal sluggishness and poor absorption, a ginger compress will help activate and restore normal functioning to the intestines. However, ginger compresses are not recommended for someone with appendicitis or pneumonia, both of which are symptoms of very excessive energy. In these cases, a cold treatment would help draw out energy and reduce overactivity. In the case of cancer, which is a symptom of very excessive energy building up in the form of actively multiplying cells, it is better not to use a ginger compress at all. If it is used, it should only be used for a few minutes to stimulate the flow of blood to and from the affected area, and then it should be immediately followed by a cold, energy-reducing plaster made with, for example, green vegetables, kombu seaweed, pearl barley, or potatoes.

Shiatsu (finger pressure) massage is similar to acupuncture in that it can have either type of effect. Shiatsu can be used to either actively stimulate and supply energy to the body or to draw out excess energy and calm the body. The way shiatsu affects the body depends largely on the condition of the practitioner. If the person giving the massage eats a lot of animal foods and sweets, drinks too much liquid, or overeats in general, his energy will be overactive and it will be difficult for him to practice negatively-charged, energy-calming shiatsu. However, if his condition is well-balanced and his understanding is good, he can use shiatsu for either purpose.

Healing With Touch

Palm healing, or te-ate *as it is known in Japan, is the most basic way to heal with energy. The basic technique is so simple that anyone can learn to do it. To begin, to generate healing power, simply sit with a straight but relaxed posture and your hands in the prayer position. Sit quietly for several minutes and allow the energy to flow between your left and right palms and the fingertips of each hand. Soon your palms will become very warm and full of ki.*

Then gently apply one palm to your right eye and breathe deeply and slowly for several minutes. Uncover the eye and compare the feeling in your two eyes. After this simple palm healing, your right eye will feel much lighter and brighter, while the left eye still feels somewhat heavy.

You can also use the same treatment on other people. The kidneys and intestines are commonly troubled areas and respond very well to this simple but powerful healing. Generally, you can lightly apply one palm to the troubled area and touch the floor with the other to "ground" your flow of healing ki. Breathe with the person you are treating, and keep your hands in position for five to ten minutes. The person receiving the treatment should relax completely.

The best palm healing is done when the energies of heaven and Earth flow freely through the person giving the treatment. A diet based on whole grains, beans, fresh local vegetables, sea vegetables, and other complex carbohydrate foods promotes a smooth and steady flow of energy and helps facilitate calming yet effective palm healing.

MATTER EQUALS SPIRIT

The philosopher Democritus was a respected thinker in ancient Greece. He was born around 460 B.C. and was called the laughing philosopher. Democritus understood that life consists of both material and non-material aspects. After separating life into the material and non-material, he concentrated on the material world and came to the conclusion that the essence of matter, or the smallest unit of matter, is the atom. However, as he continued his search for the basic building blocks of the physical world, he lost sight of, and eventually abandoned, the invisible world of energy or spirit.

That was the beginning of modern science and medicine. And so, thousands of years after Democritus, science is the science of matter. And modern scientists find it very difficult to understand spiritual things, or imagination, or the universe in its entirety. They see only what is within the realm of the senses, or in other words, what can be weighed, measured, or quantified in the form of grams, centimeters, or seconds. However, without an understanding of the invisible world of energy or spirit, we can never know the real secrets or whole meaning of life.

Scientists understand solids, liquids, gases, and some waves only because these things can be perceived by the senses or registered by machines. But things that cannot be identified in this way—which is everything beyond the range of our senses—are beyond the scope of modern science. Many scientists believe that such things cannot exist. These opinions are based on a narrow view of life and cannot lead to individual happiness or to health or peace for the world.

If Democritus and his students had seen—instead of this separation, instead of this dualism—that everything is related, or in other words, if they had had a more monistic view, their influence on the modern world would have been much different.

But despite this, several thousand years later, at the peak of material civilization, atomic physics reached the conclusion anyway that matter is equal to energy. First elements, then atoms, and finally electrons, protons, and other preatomic particles were discovered and analyzed. And when electrons were observed up close, it was discovered that they are composed of energy; they are actually masses of energy and are not solid at all. Material things are nothing but masses of energy that are constantly vibrating and changing. Moreover, matter is continually condensing out of energy and decomposing back into energy.

The world of non-matter is huge in comparison to the world of matter. All living things, including plants, animals, and human beings, are transformations of energy, as are inorganic objects. When we view life from this perspective, it becomes much easier to understand the material world, much easier to understand the human body, and much easier to live peacefully and healthfully on this Earth. However, if we think of life as only a combination of atoms and molecules, it is so difficult to find peace and happiness or to know our ultimate origin and destiny.

Even though modern civilization places great value on material things, humanity's new frontier lies beyond the world of matter in the invisible realms of mind and spirit. Thousands of years ago, ancient people discovered the unity between life and energy, physical and spiritual, mind and body. Their world view was based on an awareness of the universal forces that create all life, and their perceptions are now being confirmed by science. The meeting of these opposite-yet-complementary ways of looking at the world could lead to a future in which humanity is guided by a more universal understanding of life.

In June 1978, Mrs. Montserrat Batllori of Barcelona, Spain, after watching a beautiful sunset through her window, obtained a camera and went outside to take a picture of it. When the photo was developed, she noticed she had captured three brilliantly golden luminous energy sources over the darkly silhouetted buildings.

3.

Modern Alchemy

The whirling bubble on the surface of a brook admits us to the se-
cret of the mechanics of the sky. Every shell on the beach is a key
to it. A little water made to rotate in a cup explains the forma-
tion of the simpler shells; the addition of matter from year to year
arrives at last at the most complex forms; and yet so poor is na-
ture with all her craft, that from the beginning to the end of the
universe she has but one stuff,—but one stuff with its two ends,
to serve up all her dream-like variety.

Ralph Waldo Emerson
Nature

During the 1600s, it was discovered that the atmosphere, which
is composed mostly of gas, has weight. One of Galileo's associates, a scientist named Evangelista Torricelli, invented a device
that demonstrates the existence of air pressure. Torricelli filled a
thirty-inch glass tube with mercury and placed it straight up-
side-down with its open end in a dish. Some of the mercury
from the tube ran into the dish, but the vast majority of it
stayed in the tube.

Torricelli guessed that the Earth's atmosphere was pushing
down on the mercury in the dish, which was causing the rest of
the mercury to remain up in the tube. His device came to be
known as a barometer and is still used today to measure atmospheric pressure.

In France, an investigator named Blaise Pascal performed an
experiment similar to Torricelli's, but with a glass tube that was
forty-six feet long. Pascal discovered that the pressure of the atmosphere supports a column of water thirty-three feet high. He
also discovered that atmospheric pressure varies according to
the altitude at which the measurement is taken. He placed a

barometer at the top of a mountain in central France and found that the column there was about three inches lower than that of a barometer placed at sea level.

Mountain ranges are pushed up by the action of Earth's more-yin, expanding energy. Expansive force becomes greater the higher we rise above the Earth's surface, and the pressure of the atmosphere becomes less. On the other hand, heaven's downward or centripetal force becomes stronger as we approach the center of the Earth. As a result, atmospheric pressure becomes greater at lower altitudes. For example, pressure is far greater under the ocean than at sea level, and it increases with depth.

ANCIENT ORIGINS

An understanding of the dynamics that exist between heaven and Earth—or yang and yin—was central to the cosmologies and sciences of the ancient world. Traces of this understanding can still be found throughout the world. For example, in California, there is an unusual place with a strange and mysterious name. When Spanish explorers arrived in California, the Indians who were living near there told them it was called Inyo. In this place is found Mount Whitney, the highest mountain in the United States outside of Alaska, together with Death Valley, which is further below sea level than any other place in North America. Remarkably, the term *in* is the Japanese word for yin, while *yo* is Japanese for yang. The people who named Inyo were evidently aware that mountains represent Earth's more-yin, expanding force, while valleys are created by heaven's descending force. These two geological formations present a striking contrast between expansion and contraction, or yin and yang. This ancient name has survived until the present, and today this region is known as Inyo County, California. The name also suggests that there were exchanges between Far Eastern and Mesoamerican cultures in ancient times.

An understanding of yin and yang also provided the backdrop for the development of science. Historians usually trace the origins of modern science to ancient Greece. However, the Greeks inherited their culture from more ancient sources, including the civilizations of Sumeria, Babylonia, and Egypt. They adapted arts and sciences such as metallurgy, astronomy, mathematics, and medicine from these older civilizations and also encountered the remnants of a very ancient cosmology that understood the universe to be governed by two primary forces or energies.

Early Greek philosophers tried to reconstruct this cosmology and explain reality in terms of some type of universal substance or energy not unlike the concept of ki found throughout Asia. For example, around 700 B.C., a Greek thinker named Anaximes stated that air is the basis of the universe and that all things move and change in cycles governed by two forces related to it: expansion, which he termed *in-breath*, and contraction, which he termed *out-breath*. Two centuries later, Heraclitus, perhaps the greatest of the pre-Socratic philosophers, stated that life and nature are part of an eternal process of change and that all things come into existence under the influence of centripetal force and decompose because of centrifugal force. He named this universal process of change *Logos*, which later became the foundation for the concept of logic, and stated that fire—or in modern terms, preatomic particles or plasma—form the basis of matter.

Empedocles, another of the early philosophers, believed that matter cycles through four stages, which he called fire, air, water, and earth. He stated that all things unite through a force he called love and separate through a force he called strife. The same as Empedocles, Aristotle believed that the world can be understood in terms of these four stages. Aristotle felt that a form of "primitive matter" is at the heart of all things and that this primitive matter exists only potentially until it takes form through a process of materialization.

Democritus, who we met in Chapter 2, proposed a view that contrasts sharply with that of Empedocles and Aristotle. He felt that the universe is composed of two fundamental components, which he termed atoms and space. He stated that atoms are indivisible units of matter. But Aristotle took issue with this theory and managed to discredit it.

As a result, the view espoused by the pre-Socratic philosophers prevailed through the Middle Ages and became one of the fundamental ideas behind the practice of alchemy, which was based on the belief that one element can be changed into another. Alchemy was widely practiced in Europe, India, China, and other parts of the world. Many of our present sciences, including chemistry, have their origin in this ancient art.

The European alchemists modified the notion of the four elements into the "doctrine of two contraries." These alchemists believed that two complementary factors—fire (yang), represented by sulphur, and water (yin), represented by mercury—come together deep within the Earth and produce either base metals or precious metals. Their practical efforts were directed toward trying to change base metals, such as mercury, into gold and other precious metals.

The same as the philosophers who preceded them, the alchemists believed that the diverse forms of matter found in nature all have a common origin. Guided by an intuitive awareness of the law of change, they believed that an element is a temporary form of a more universal energy or substance and that one element can be transmuted into another.

As time went by, however, investigators began to doubt the theoretical basis of this ancient science, especially since it was eventually interpreted to mean that the universe is literally made up of only four elements. Scientists finally abandoned this narrow interpretation and resurrected the atomic theory of Democritus. The atomic theory offered what seemed to be a plausible explanation for the underlying structure of the numerous elements that chemists were discovering. However, the concept of the atom as an absolute, indivisible unit as espoused by Democritus and later by John Dalton, a nineteenth-century English chemist, collapsed in the twentieth century with the discovery of smaller, subatomic particles. It collapsed even further with the discovery that these particles are actually condensed units of non-physical energy.

CLASSIFYING THE ELEMENTS

Yin and yang make it possible to resolve the schism between those who view matter as dynamically changing energy and those who envision it as static groupings of atoms. Let us begin with some basic classifications. Higher temperatures are more yang, while lower temperatures are more yin. Things that are small and compact are yang, while large and expanded things are yin. Things with a heavier weight are more yang, while those with a lighter weight are more yin. Things with a greater density, or with a harder and more solid structure, are more yang, while those with less density, or with a softer or more diffused form, are more yin. Red is a more yang color, while violet is more yin. (The colors of the spectrum can be classified from yang to yin as follows: red, orange, yellow, green, blue, violet.) Infrared, which we don't perceive as an actual color, is more yang than red is, while ultraviolet is more yin than violet is. These basic criteria are summarized in Table 3.1 and are sufficient to help us discover which elements are yin and which are yang.

The table of important elements (Table 3.2) shown on page 62 presents the melting and boiling points of thirty-eight of the known elements. Let us see how yin and yang can help us classify the elements using this basic information.

Atomic Mass or Weight

Atomic number refers to the number of protons in the nucleus of an atom. It also refers to the number of electrons orbiting the nucleus. *Atomic weight* refers to the weight or mass of the protons and neutrons in a nucleus. Orbiting electrons contain practically no mass and therefore have very little effect on the weight of an atom. The elements with larger atomic weights have more protons and neutrons and are thus heavier, or more yang, than the lighter elements. They are also more dense than

Table 3.1. Yang and Yin Characteristics

	Yang	Yin
Temperature	Hotter	Colder
Size	Smaller	Larger
Weight	Heavier	Lighter
Density	More dense	Less dense
Color	Red, orange, yellow, green, blue, violet	

Table 3.2. Melting and Boiling Points of Elements

Element	Melting Point °C	Boiling Point °C
Aluminum	659.7	2057
Antimony	630.5	1380
Arsenic	814	615*
Barium	850	1140
Bismuth	271.3	1560
Boron	2300	2550*
Bromine	−7.2	58.8
Calcium	842	1240
Carbon	above 3500*	4200
Chlorine	−101.6	−34.6
Chromium	1890	2480
Cobalt	1495	2900
Copper	1083	2336
Fluorine	−223	−187
Gold	1063	2600
Hydrogen	−259	−253
Iodine	113.5	184.4
Iron	1535	3000
Lead	327.4	1620
Magnesium	651	1107
Manganese	1260	1900
Mercury	−38.9	356.6
Nickel	1455	2900
Nitrogen	−209.9	−195.8
Oxygen	−218	−183
Phosphorus	44.1	280
Platinum	1773.5	4300
Potassium	62.3	760
Radium	700	1140
Silicon	1420	2355
Silver	960.8	1950
Sodium	97.5	880
Strontium	800	1150
Sulfur	114.5	444.6
Tin	231.9	2270
Titanium	1800	over 3000
Tungsten	3370	5900
Zinc	419.5	907

*Element sublimes: solid becomes gas, gas becomes solid, without first becoming liquid.

those with fewer particles in the nucleus. Greater density is a yang characteristic, while less density is yin.

Melting Point and Boiling Point

Below its melting point, an element exists in solid form. Between its melting and boiling points, it exists as a liquid, and beyond its boiling point, as a gas. Beyond the gas stage, an element exists as a plasma, which is an intermediary between the worlds of matter and energy. Beyond that, matter dissolves into vibrations, waves, or energy.

We know that the upward limit of temperature is very high, although we don't know what the actual limit is. But we do know the low temperature limit, which is –273°C., or 273 degrees below the freezing point of water, also known as absolute zero. Here on Earth, we cannot make anything colder than that. On some other planet or in some other place in the universe, we may be able to go much lower, but as far as the Earth is concerned, that so-called absolute zero is the lowest known temperature.

Water has a melting point of 0°C. and a boiling point of 100°C. Some elements have a much lower melting point and are more yin. Others have a much higher melting point and are more yang. At room temperature (about 32°C.), water exists in between the melting and boiling points, or in other words, in a liquid state. At the same time, some elements, such as iron and copper, are already frozen at this temperature, so appear solid. At room temperature, these and other solid elements exist in a crystallized form similar to that of ice. Very high temperatures are required to change them into their liquid form. Other elements, such as oxygen, nitrogen, and hydrogen, are already far above their boiling point and exist as gas at room temperature. These elements become liquid only at very cold temperatures, near absolute zero.

Although we may not notice it, all states of matter exist at the same time within our surroundings. Some elements are in a frozen or ice state; some, such as mercury, are in a semi-frozen state; some are in a liquid state; some are in a gaseous or plasmic state; and others exist potentially as waves or vibrations.

Modern civilization deals mostly with matter in the frozen (solid) and liquid states and is not concerned much with matter in the gaseous, plasmic, and vibrational states. As a result, our view of life tends to revolve around solid matter while ignoring these other dimensions of reality.

Size

Small atoms (those with few protons, electrons, and neutrons) are more yang, while large ones (those with a greater number of preatomic particles) are more yin. With one proton and one electron, hydrogen is the smallest atom. In terms of size, it is very yang. As we go higher in atomic number, the atoms get larger, with more preatomic particles, and become progressively more yin. This classification is the opposite of the classification by weight: as atoms become heavier, they become more yang. Yin and yang always exist together and balance each other out. The elements are electrically neutral because the number of positively charged protons in each nucleus is counterbalanced by the number of negatively charged electrons orbiting at the periphery. As the elements become larger (more yin), they also become increasingly dense or heavy (more yang).

Color and Wavelength

When we burn an element and put a prism in front of it, we see certain colors emitted more strongly than others. This is called spectroscopic examination. Examining the color spectrum of each element adds another dimension to our classification and facilitates the arrangement of the elements in a spiral with seven orbits (see Figure 3.1).

In this arrangement, the light elements (those with small atomic numbers) are positioned at the periphery and the heavy elements (those with large atomic numbers) are toward the center. The atoms become progressively heavier toward the center of the spiral. The elements in the lower half of each orbit emit more yang colors, with longer spectroscopic wavelengths (measured in angstrom units), while those in the upper half emit more yin colors, with shorter wavelengths.

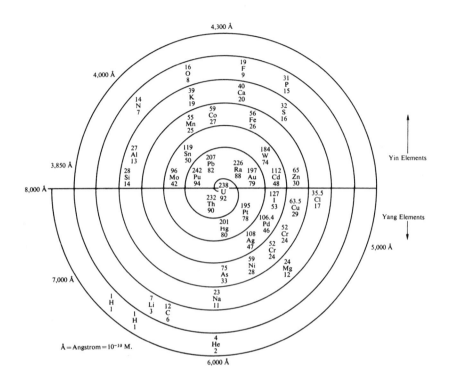

Figure 3.1.   The spiral arrangement of the elements.

We can discover many interesting things in Figure 3.1. For example, oxygen is in a more-yin position and carbon occupies a more-yang position. (We can confirm these classifications by checking the melting and boiling points of these elements on Table 3.2 on page 62.) Carbon and oxygen are like male and female: they have nearly opposite tendencies and combine very easily. Oxygen and hydrogen are also far from each other on the chart and combine very easily, as they do in water. The strong attraction between these oppositely charged elements is one reason water exists in such abundance, covering more than three-fourths of the Earth's surface and making up more than 60 percent of the weight of the human body.

This spiral arrangement of the elements can help solve all of the mysteries in the field of chemistry, such as why certain elements combine easily and others don't. It can also help us figure out why certain compounds are fairly common, while others are rare. And, as we will see below, the spiral additionally offers us a clue to how the elements originally came into being.

NEW TECHNOLOGIES

The invention of the steam engine in the 1700s triggered the Industrial Revolution. The steam engine was invented by James Watt. One day, Watt was sitting in the kitchen watching a kettle of water starting to boil. He noticed the lid moving up and down and thought, "If we use this steam as an applied force, we can generate tremendous power." This thinking led to the invention of the steam engine and to the development of modern industry.

However, if Watt had known yin and yang, he could have made a far greater contribution. Which is more yang: water or steam? The water in his tea kettle was more yang, especially the water at the bottom of the pot. Watt was only using his sense of sight, so he observed the steam's action and simply imitated that. If he had used more intuitive understanding, he would have paid attention to the more yang part.

Because it is diffused, steam is actually more inefficient than hot water. A simple experiment can confirm this.

Fill a test tube part way with water and plug it with a cork. Then heat it over a candle or gas burner. When the water begins to boil, the steam will pop the cork. This confirms Watt's principle of steam power. Now refill and recork the tube, and apply the heat again. This time, though, just before the water starts to boil, tilt the tube sideways so the water runs downward and touches the cork. The hot water will blow the cork off.

This simple experiment shows that steam engines waste energy. Steam requires much more heating time and fuel than hot water and gives off less power. A machine that utilizes the power of hot water would be much stronger and more efficient than a steam engine.

Many modern inventions are equally inefficient. They often waste a tremendous amount of energy in the form of the

Earth's natural resources and pollute the environment. They are created out of mechanical thinking and do not reflect an understanding of yin and yang. Moreover, if you carefully examine all of our modern scientific laws, discoveries, theories, and so forth, you will discover that many of them are really superstitious assumptions. Most will probably be naturally changed or discarded in ten, fifty, or a hundred years from now.

Newton's theory of gravity, although widely accepted as the foundation of modern science, offers an example. According to the famous story, Newton was sitting under a tree and saw an apple fall to the ground. When he saw the apple fall, he thought, "Aha! Maybe the Earth is pulling it down." This was the beginning of the theory of gravity.

But that idea ran directly counter to Christianity, which stated that God created the Earth. If Newton had stood far away, he might have thought, "No, maybe the heavens are pushing the apple down." Heaven's force is actually pushing apples and other objects to the Earth's surface and is also pushing the Earth itself, as well as all the other planets, around the Sun in spirals. "God created the Earth" means that from the periphery of space, or infinity, heaven's force spirals inward and creates all material phenomena.

But Newton didn't think this way. He thought that everything had a center, like the Earth, and that this center pulled everything toward it. This idea corresponds to materialism, or the notion that the purpose of life is to try to pull as many material objects as possible into one's orbit in order to accumulate them. Newton's theory provided scientific justification for such problematic behaviors as egoism and self-centered individualism, as well as for unbridled materialism, and gave further credence to the idea of independent national sovereignty. This superstitious view also separated people from their intuitive awareness of God, or infinity, as the universal source of life, energy, and matter, so that the church and science split further apart.

THE EVOLUTION OF THE ELEMENTS

The first eight elements on the Periodic Table of the Elements are like the basic octave of the musical scale (see Figure 3.2).

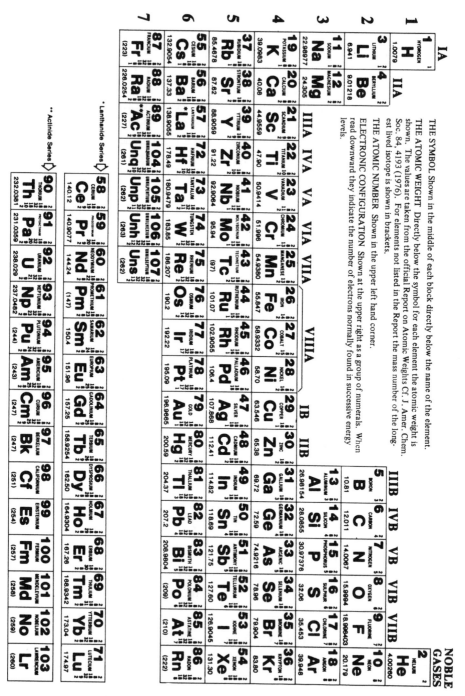

THE SYMBOL Shown in the middle of each block directly below the name of the element.

THE ATOMIC WEIGHT Directly below the symbol for each element the atomic weight is shown. The values are taken from the official Report on Atomic Weights Cf. J. Amer. Chem. Soc. 84, 4193 (1976). For elements not listed in the Report the mass number of the long-est lived isotope is shown in brackets.

THE ATOMIC NUMBER Shown in the upper left hand corner.

ELECTRONIC CONFIGURATION Shown at the upper right as a group of numerals. When read downward they indicate the number of electrons normally found in successive energy levels.

Figure 3.2. Periodic Chart of the Elements.

Similar to the alternating tones of music, certain of these elements are more yin and others are more yang. Helium, lithium, beryllium, and boron are not found much on the Earth's surface, but hydrogen, oxygen, carbon, and nitrogen are found in abundance. Among these four common elements, hydrogen and carbon form a more yang group, while nitrogen and oxygen form a more yin group. As you can imagine, the elements in these complementary groups combine very easily with each other. When oxygen, which is yin, combines with hydrogen and carbon, the result is a carbohydrate molecule. When these elements combine with nitrogen, protein molecules result. These chemical combinations provide the basis for all life on Earth.

Common sense tells us that the 107 elements discovered on the Earth so far did not just suddenly appear—one day oxygen, one day nitrogen, the next day platinum, and so forth. The elements are linked by a continual process, forming an evolutionary continuum. A fish and a human being appear to be different, but we know they are connected and are both a part of one evolutionary chain. In the same way, we know, one process must be linking hydrogen and iron, nitrogen and gold, silicon and sodium, and all of the chemical elements. Science has merely to yet discover this evolutionary process, primarily because of the belief that one element cannot change into another element under natural conditions.

The process in which one element changes into another is totally different from what occurs when two or more atoms mix together but each retains its own nature, which is known as chemical combination. It also differs from the change of state in which elements pass from solid to liquid to gas. In this evolutionary process, two elements overlap, merge their electrons into a single set, and become a totally different element. According to modern physics, transmutation of elements occurs only at a very high temperature and pressure, and under conditions of intense energy, such as those generated in a cyclotron or atomic reactor.

Hydrogen (H) is the first and most basic element. It contains one proton and one electron. It represents the original form that energy takes when it evolves from a vibrational state toward condensed energetic particles, which in reality are simply very compact clouds or spirals of energy and not discrete units of matter. Hydrogen has an atomic number (the number of protons and also the number of electrons) of 1 and an atomic weight (the number of protons and neutrons in the nucleus) of 1. The most basic form of hydrogen contains one electron and one proton.

Hydrogen combines with "heavy" hydrogen (hydrogen-3), an isotope that contains two neutrons and one proton, to create helium (He). This occurs according to the formula: $H^1_1 + H^1_3 = He^2_4$.

Lithium (Li), the next element on the periodic table, arises when an atom of helium combines with an atom of hydrogen-3 according to the formula: $He^2_4 + H^1_3 = Li^3_7$. Then an atom of lithium combines with an atom of semi-heavy hydrogen (hydrogen-2, or deuterium), which has one neutron, to make beryllium (Be) according to the formula: $Li^3_7 + H^1_2 = Be^4_9$. The remaining elements in the primary group are created through the following transmutations: $He^2_4 + Li^3_7 = B^5_{11}$, or alternatively $Be^4_9 + H^1_2 = B^5_{11}$, for boron; $B^5_{11} + H^1_1 = C^6_{12}$ for carbon; $C^6_{12} + H^1_2 = N^7_{14}$ for nitrogen; and $N^7_{14} + H^1_2 = O^8_{16}$ or $C^6_{12} + He^2_4 = O^8_{16}$ for oxygen.

The evolution of the elements continues beyond the initial eight, in higher octaves, so to speak, until we arrive at the very heavy elements, such as lead and gold. As the elements become heavier and more complex, there are several possible roots or pathways for their creation. Each of these different pathways creates a slightly different quality of the new element. For example, the oxygen produced by the combination of nitrogen and hydrogen differs slightly from that created by the combination of carbon and helium.

Meanwhile, as we enter the central region of the spiral, a reverse process also takes place since yang always changes into yin and yin always changes back into yang. As we reach the elements with the very heavy atomic weights of 200, 230, and so on, such as radium and uranium, what kind of character arises? A radioactive character, with the heavier elements changing back into lighter ones. Elements are constantly changing back and forth, not only in different chemical combinations and states of matter, but also in terms of their position within the spiral of evolution.

Now, under what circumstances does natural transmutation occur? First, we know that two combining elements need to be complementary—one yin and the other yang. Second, in order for atomic fusion to take place, the central nuclei of the combining elements need to be in a more fragile, plasmic state. Atoms change more easily in this condition. You can picture this by imagining two big galaxies swerving toward each other, one spiraling clockwise and the other, counterclockwise. They come closer and closer, and then fuse into a new galaxy.

Nuclear fusion is similar to what happens during sex. As I explain in the book *The Gentle Art of Making Love*, a man's energy spirals counterclockwise and a woman's energy spirals clockwise. As the lovemaking intensifies, each person heats up until he or she reaches a very energized state similar to plasma. At this point, orgasm occurs, followed by the potential fusion of egg and sperm. The transmutation of elements occurs through the same type of fusion that creates a new human life.

SPIRALS WITHIN SPIRALS

One question that occurs to many people when they encounter the spiral of the elements is, Why does hydrogen, which is classified as a yang element, occupy the most peripheral, or yin, position on the chart? Hydrogen is very small. Centripetal force, or pressure from the outside, comes into it with tremendous velocity. We can observe the same thing in the solar system. Pluto is tiny and very yang, yet it occupies the most yin, or peripheral, position of the nine known planets.

Hydrogen also exists at the center of another spiral—the huge spiral of preatomic formation. Not long ago, scientists discovered electrons in the nucleus of atoms! This completely upset thirty years of conventional study, since according to the modern view, electrons and protons occupy fixed positions within the atom. According to our thinking as presented here, however, atoms are formed spirally, and after billions of years, their electrons change into protons. The nucleus is the condensation and accumulation of electrons and other peripheral particles. It represents the very yang conclusion of the spiral of preatomic evolution.

Now you can see the symphony of the universe: a prelude, seven movements of a main composition, and a grand finale. The first octave or eight elements—hydrogen, helium, lithium, beryllium, boron, carbon, nitrogen, and oxygen—represent the prelude. Among these eight, the greatest antagonism is between carbon and oxygen, which together produce silicon (Si). This combination produces seven movements in the world of matter: $C + O = Si$, $2(C + O) = Iron (Fe)$, and so on, until $7(C + O) = Platinum (Pt)$.

Platinum is the last of the metallic elements. The finale is a dissolution, the diminishing melodies that begin with gold and mercury, and culminate with the radioactive elements.

The conclusion of the preatomic world becomes the beginning or periphery of the next, the atomic world. The spiral of elements is also at the periphery of a huge biological spiral,

Scientists Tackle Spiral Riddle

Los Angeles (UPI)—DNA, the master molecule of life, is a spiraling ladder loaded with the hereditary characters that determine everything from the color of eyes to the shape of a leaf. On a larger scale, spirals are the shapes of whirlpools and tornadoes, and on Jupiter, a spiral is the form of the whirling Great Red Spot.

Scientists, mindful that galaxies, the most titanic spirals of all, did not take shape by accident, now think they were formed by electromagnetic forces that whipped cosmic matter into one of the most widely repeated forms in nature. "Vortices," theoretical physicist Anthony Peratt said of spiral shapes, "are important in nature from the smallest imaginable to the largest. Water draining from a bathtub forms a vortex. Vortices are morphologies (structures) that can be seen everywhere." (March 30, 1988.)

Used with permission.

which begins with viruses and bacteria, grows into cells, and proceeds toward the creation of man. This is the order of the universe—spirals within spirals, manifolds of spirals. The governing principle of each of these worlds is therefore the same: centripetality and centrifugality, or yang and yin.

The biological spiral is itself on the periphery of a huge social and historical spiral. If present science discovers this enormous principle, everything can be united. Now, psychology, biology, religion, and technology are all separate, with hundreds of laws and theories in each discipline. This unifying principle could bring them all together and make them into one, embracing and understanding the laws of change.

BIOLOGICAL TRANSMUTATIONS

Nearly thirty years ago, Aveline and I were living in New York. I lectured every week on different aspects of macrobiotics, and George Ohsawa, who had been our teacher in Japan, also visited from time to time to give seminars. One summer evening after a lecture, a group of us went with Mr. Ohsawa to a macrobiotic restaurant in the city. Several friends brought along a newspaper clipping about the work of a French doctor named Louis Kervran. According to the article, Dr. Kervran had recently presented the idea that sodium and potassium change into each other under certain natural conditions.

Mr. Ohsawa was delighted with this discovery since he had been teaching for many years that the number one principle of life is that everything is constantly changing. He envisioned the material world not as static and absolute, but as ephemeral and changing. He stated that for a modern scientist to have found the principle of change in the world of elements was indeed a monumental discovery.

Soon afterward, Mr. Ohsawa was lecturing in Paris and mentioned Professor Kervran's discovery. He stated that it is in accord with the macrobiotic cosmology of change. After the lecture, many people came up to him to say hello, and finally an elderly gentleman who had been standing behind everyone else came up to shake hands. The gentleman said, "I am Dr. Kervran." Mr. Ohsawa was so happy.

Mr. Ohsawa and Dr. Kervran met several days later to exchange ideas. Professor Kervran mentioned that he had not yet disclosed all of the details about his discoveries and that he was facing a great deal of criticism and opposition from the scientific community. Mr. Ohsawa encouraged him to be patient and suggested that he write a book. Kervran left the meeting feeling inspired and uplifted, and went on to write a book entitled *Transmutations Biologique,* or *Biological Transmutations.*

Kervran had discovered biological transmutations while working as a doctor for the French government on a construction project in the Sahara desert. Every day, he analyzed what the construction workers ate and also what they excreted. The results of his analyses were puzzling. With certain elements, the quantities being discharged were not equal to those being consumed. The workers were discharging more of some elements than they were taking in, and less of other elements. Kervran then selected two major elements—sodium and potassium—for further study.

In the biological world, the ratio between sodium and potassium is crucial. More than 100 years ago, a Japanese doctor named Sagen Ishizuka had discovered the importance of these elements in the human body. He found that they function in a complementary and antagonistic way in the body and that if the ratio between them is kept within a certain range, the body remains healthy. He believed that the ideal ratio between sodium and potassium is about one to five.

Dr. Ishizuka used the terms yin and yang to describe the functioning of these elements. He stated that sodium represents the primary force of contraction (yang) in the body, while potassium represents expansion (yin). Mr. Ohsawa later assimilated Ishizuka's theory and broadened it into a comprehensive teaching about the role of food in health. He proved it extensively by helping thousands of people recover from sickness through a naturally balanced diet. Since then, I have modified Mr. Ohsawa's concept somewhat to include not only sodium and potassium, but also the many other yin and yang elements found in the body. I have found that on the whole, the yin group of elements, represented by potassium, and the yang group of elements, represented by sodium, generally balance out according to a flexible ratio that averages about seven to one.

Dr. Kervran discovered that the French laborers in the Sahara were eliminating less sodium and more potassium than they were taking in. After rechecking his data, he came to the conclusion that the sodium was changing into potassium in their bodies, under the conditions of relatively low temperature, pressure, and energy.

If we subtract the atomic number and weight of sodium (Na) from those of potassium (K), we can discover which of the other elements is required for this transmutation to take place. The process of subtraction yields the following formula: K^{19}_{39} − $Na^{11}_{23} = O^{8}_{16}$. Oxygen, coming from the air we breathe, combines in the human body with sodium from salt and certain foods, and changes into potassium. Kervran theorized that the following factors contributed to the process of transmutation among the French laborers:

- They worked very hard, so their energy levels were especially high.

- Hard physical labor caused their metabolism and breathing to accelerate, resulting in an increased supply of oxygen.

- Hard labor caused them to sweat, and they took in extra sodium in the form of salt tablets.

- Working under the hot desert sun made their body temperature rise, which accelerated the process of transmutation.

Although Mr. Ohsawa and Dr. Kervran wanted to test this theory, neither of them had the technical expertise to design an experiment. But Mr. Ohsawa thought back to when he was a young student attending the Sorbonne in Paris. At that time, he had made friends with a man named Neven Henaff, who later went on to become a brilliant chemist. Ohsawa told Kervran that Dr. Henaff would be able to help them and that he would try to locate him.

After searching for almost a year, Mr. Ohsawa finally found Henaff and brought him to New York. Henaff began working every day on translating Dr. Kervran's book into English, and the three of us met daily to discuss how to set up an experiment.

Then Mr. Ohsawa had to return to Japan, and Henaff went along. The two men continued trying to figure out there how to design the experiment, but couldn't find a solution. Eventually, Henaff left the project for personal reasons.

After Henaff left, Mr. Ohsawa wrote to me and said, "From today I will go on diet number seven [a whole grain fast] until I discover the solution." I don't know if he ever really went on diet number seven or not, but I sent back a letter saying, "Bravo!"

Two weeks later, I received a special delivery letter from George Ohsawa marked, "Urgent." In it, he said, "I have discovered a way to do it!" He explained that while he had been asleep one night, he had had a dream. In the dream, from the darkness of the sky, a big hand had stretched out; every time it stretched out, thunder and lightning shot from the fingers. While this was happening in the sky, on the surface of the Earth, various elements began to arise, creating the beginnings of life. He said he interpreted the dream to mean that electromagnetic current—symbolized by the thunder and the lightning—was necessary to stimulate the elements to change into one another.

In the Laboratory

The next morning, Mr. Ohsawa called Professor Masashiro Torii and several other Japanese friends who were scientists and asked for their help in setting up some very simple equipment. With their help, he designed an experiment that would simulate the spiral of materialization through which the world of matter comes into being. In this never-ending process, one infinity polarizes into yin and yang, which in turn produce energy or vibrations, preatomic particles such as protons and electrons, elements, plants, and ultimately animal life, including man. (This process is symbolized in the book of Genesis by the story of the seven days of creation.) Mr. Ohsawa believed that in order to make elements, they needed to duplicate the first several stages of this process.

Guided by Mr. Ohsawa, the Japanese team used a vacuum tube to simulate infinity, or non-being, and attached positively and negatively charged electrodes to either end of it to simulate yin and yang. The electrodes were made of copper and iron.

When the experiment was underway, the electrodes would be charged with an electrical current to simulate the world of vibration or energy. The men then filled the tube with sodium and attached a valve to it to let in air (oxygen) at the right time. They placed a spectroscope prism and screen in front of it to monitor the experiment. They finished setting up everything at about midnight and planned to return the following morning to see if it would work.

That night, however, the professor whose laboratory they were using became curious. He simply couldn't wait until the next day, so went back to the lab and started the experiment. He applied electricity to the sodium for more than twenty minutes, until it became very hot and expanded. Finally, a clear band of orange appeared on the screen. He then opened the valve and let oxygen enter the tube. The screen went black, and in less than a second, a band of pure blue (the color of potassium) appeared.

He immediately telephoned Mr. Ohsawa. A short while later, the entire team gathered at the lab and repeated the experiment—and again, the orange band disappeared, only to be replaced by blue a moment later. To confirm their results, the men ran a complete analysis on the new element and found that it was in fact potassium. The date was June 21, 1964.

Non-Rusting Iron

The first eight elements are the ancestors of those that follow them on the spiral of evolution. All other elements are created from these eight. Among the basic eight, carbon and oxygen have the greatest polarity and hence the greatest attraction. It is through their combination that practically all of the heavier elements come about. Of course, other light elements also combine with each other, but the combination of carbon and oxygen is the most common.

When one atom of carbon (C^6_{12}) fuses with an atom of oxygen (O^8_{16}), the product is an atom of silicon (Si^{14}_{28}). Because this bond is so strong, silicon is a very hard, stable element. If two atoms of carbon combine with two atoms of oxygen— $2(C^6_{12} + O^8_{16})$—the new element X^{28}_{56} is created, which exists within the iron family of elements. Iron (Fe) has an atomic weight of 56, while nickel (Ni), also a member of the iron family, has an atomic number of 28. Cobalt (Co), which is also part of the iron family, is in between: Fe^{26}_{56}, Co^{27}_{59}, Ni^{28}_{59}. So the combination of two atoms of carbon and two atoms of oxygen creates an element in the iron family which, our research team was to discover, has a number of special properties.

We then set up another experiment using only carbon and oxygen. We used a carbon rod as one electrode, and placed carbon powder in a carbon crucible. We put the crucible on a metal plate that also served as the other electrode. We positioned the end of the carbon rod in the middle of the powder, then passed electricity through the powder and let oxygen from the air combine with it.

A brown-black metallic powder formed at the bottom of the crucible. We tested the powder by several methods—including magnetic inspection, spectroscopic and chemical analysis, and examination by reagent—and found that it contained iron, cobalt, and nickel. A variety of other elements was also present due to the fusion of other gases, including nitrogen and hydrogen, from the air.

However, in order to produce high grade steel, it is necessary to make the conditions of the experiment very exact, for example by applying a specific amount of electricity and controlling how other elements from the air combine with the carbon and oxygen. But these technical considerations are minor compared with the magnitude of achieving the atomic transmutation under normal laboratory conditions. If the technical details can be worked out and the procedure adapted on a large scale, the complicated process of mining and refining iron ore would become unnecessary. Steel could become very inexpensive, perhaps as little as 1 percent of its present cost.

In addition to the effort involved in producing it, modern steel has another drawback: it rusts very easily. The huge steel ships sitting in the harbor must be constantly scraped and repainted, while the rust pollutes the water. On the other hand, iron that is made through the fusion of carbon and oxygen is very strong. It does not attract additional oxygen and consequently doesn't rust or oxidize.

Iron poles have been discovered in New Delhi, India, and Bonn, West Germany, standing one and a half meters above the ground and twenty-five meters below. Local legends say they were installed a long time ago, and nobody knows their purpose. Although they are centuries old, these poles have not rusted. Their non-rusting quality is similar to that of the iron produced in our experiments. Could people long ago have discovered how to transmute the atom?

AN ALCHEMIST'S DREAM

In the Orient, there are old stories of people called the Sen-Nin. As we said in Chapter 2, the Sen-Nin lived in the mountains, developing their cosmological understanding and realization of health, longevity, and physical, mental, and spiritual freedom. Perhaps you've seen pictures of wise old men with large beards and strong eyes. The Sen-Nin were something like that, or like Yoda in *The Empire Strikes Back*—a wise old man with unusual powers.

These legends also say that these men made gold. They say their school of instruction had four stages:

1. Self-mastery.
2. Longevity (not only 70 or 80 years, but 100, 200, 300 years, free from sickness).
3. Educating and guiding others.
4. Alchemy.

When they discovered how to make gold, the stories say they were graduates.

Of course, there was no university or actual school for learning these things. The mountains themselves were the school. The Sen-Nin lived in the mountains for many years, eating wild buckwheat, tree bark, and wild grasses; meditating; exercising; and gradually figuring out and mastering each of the levels.

According to legend, they made gold from mercury. Gold has an atomic weight of 197 and mercury, the next element on the periodic table, has an atomic weight of 200. How did the Sen-Nin know that a silver semi-solid–semi-liquid element and a soft yellow metal were so close to each other on the periodic table?

The ancient method practiced by the Sen-Nin must have been different than that used in our experiments. Our method was based on combining two lighter elements to produce a heavier one. Theirs was based on subtracting some element from mercury in order to produce gold. If we check the periodic table, we see that gold (Au) can be produced by subtracting an atom of hydrogen-3 from mercury (Hg): $Hg^{80}_{200} - H^1_3 = Au^{79}_{197}$. On his final visit to America, Mr. Ohsawa said to me, "Michio, we must discover this reduction method if we wish to make gold." He died soon after that.

THE TRANSMUTATION OF SOCIETY

When the Sen-Nin mastered a problem, they did not hold on to the solution. They didn't tell anyone about it or write it down, but let it be forgotten again. For them, such things were simply a part of their self-development and training to understand and gain mastery over the material world.

Today, however, we are facing a global environmental crisis that is threatening the future of our planet. Global warming, the depletion of the ozone layer, and the accumulation of toxic materials in the soil, water, and air are only a few of the problems that are confronting us as we approach the twenty-first century.

As we saw in the example of the steam engine, modern technology is often wasteful and inefficient. It depletes our non-renewable resources and pollutes the environment. The Earth's non-renewable resources are like the principal in a bank account: they exist in finite quantities. When we live off our principal, we eventually go bankrupt. But this is exactly what modern civilization is doing.

Atomic transmutation, or modern alchemy, can help us develop technologies that are truly self-sustaining. It can make a practically unlimited supply of materials readily available. If iron, gold, copper, and other elements can be produced at low

Clean Energy

Within all types of energy on the Earth are just two basic primary currents: the centripetal energy raining down upon us, generated by the infinite cosmos, and centrifugal energy, generated by the Earth's rotation. We refer to these two currents as heaven's force and Earth's force.

These two currents create all other types of energy, such as sunlight, wind, fire, electricity, gas, petroleum, coal, and atomic energy. Every possible form of fuel or energy we could use on this Earth is nothing but a by-product or transformation of the two original forces.

"Clean" or "efficient" energy simply means heaven's and Earth's forces used as directly as possible, with their indirect by-products used as little as possible.

A plant is a fairly direct form of heaven's and Earth's energies, particularly if it is allowed to grow naturally and without much interference or "protection" from the environment. Within less than a year, for example, heaven and Earth create a tall cereal plant from a tiny grain. Stone and metal, by contrast, are created by a much longer and more indirect process.

Ancient people relied much more on plant foods than on animal products, which are a less direct form of nutritional energy. It takes much less energy to produce food for a vegetarian population than it does for a meat-eating society. Moreover, by cutting tropical rain forests to provide grazing land for cattle, we are diminishing the range of biodiversity on the planet and contributing to the buildup of carbon dioxide in the atmosphere.

Among the edible plants, cereal grains use the most direct combination of heaven's and Earth's forces. The ancient people who built stone circles, shrines, temples, and other structures along the currents of Earth's energy of course ate whole grains as their staple foods. Vegetables, which represent relatively more heaven's force in the case of roots and more Earth's force in the case of leafy greens, were secondary. Animal foods, which represent a very indirect transformation of these natural energies, were relied on as seldom as possible.

The macrobiotic diet applies the principle of clean energy to the selection and preparation of food, using maximum efficiency; using less animal foods, oils, and fat; using less elaborate processing technologies and only very simple preparations; relying on cereal grains; and minimizing or avoiding the use of chemical fertilizers and pesticides. Our bodies, therefore, naturally become clean and energized when we eat this way.

cost and in practically unlimited quantities from air, water, and soil, civilization can prosper without depleting the planet's reserves or polluting the environment.

As we discover ways to make steel and other basic materials from lighter elements in the air, water, and soil, then like the Sen-Nin, we will be able to graduate to the next level. Because all elements ultimately come from the world of waves or vibration, it may become possible to produce them directly from pure energy.

If we develop to this level, humanity will have achieved a truly spiritual civilization. At that time, not only will solutions to the environmental crisis be apparent, but we will have gained the ability to control the material world and play with it freely according to our image and dream.

4.

Past Lives, Future Lives

Cool things become warm, the warm grows cool; the moist dries, the parched becomes moist. Immortals become mortals, mortals become immortals; they live in each other's death and die in each other's life.

From the *Fragments*
of Heraclitus

When people speak of "mind and body" or of "spirit and matter," they are usually speaking of our bodies and all things that we can detect with our senses as constituting the material world and being separate from, and independent of, the spiritual world, which includes everything from higher vibrations to infinity. These are thought of as two separate worlds.

People who tend to be concerned with material things while ignoring the other world often forget that the higher world exists. These people we call materialists. Other people have the opposite tendency, which is to ignore material reality and emphasize the invisible world. Those people we call spiritualists.

These two types of thinking are created by the different vibrational influences people receive according to where they live. As we saw in Chapter 2, Earth's rotation is creating an expanding current of centrifugal force that arises most strongly at the equator. Therefore, people who live closer to the equator than to a pole—for example, in India—receive more of this force, so their thinking naturally has an upward, expanding tendency. Forgetting about the condensed physical world, they naturally emphasize the importance of the stars and the heavens, of vibrations and spirit. On the other hand, people who live nearer to one of the poles receive more of the condensing influence of heaven's force. Naturally, their thinking tends to be materially oriented, with emphasis on the tangible world that is here and now.

Modern civilization has been generated by this second type of thinking, which generally comes from the countries in northern Europe. Meanwhile, various religions and spiritual techniques generated by countries more influenced by the opposite tendency have recently been introduced into this materialistic civilization. One naturally attracts the other to make balance.

Although they are balancing each other out, it is still not an ideal situation since both sides are continuing to be one-sided in their approach, thinking either, "Money is valueless; only spiritual enlightenment is important," or "Spirituality is a waste of time; material success is all that matters." This view, whether spiritually or materially oriented, is called dualism. In reality, spiritual phenomena and material phenomena are nothing but two manifestations of a single process. For example, physical health is equivalent to spiritual health, and vice versa. If we see these two as separate, if we look at them with the eyes of dualism, then we will never achieve health in either world. In this universe, spirit is always changing into matter and matter back into spirit. The two are simply the front and back of one universe. Let us now examine how this endless process of transformation takes place.

OUR SPIRITUAL JOURNEY

Human life arises from the world of plants or, you may say, from the vegetable kingdom. Our bodies are created through the transformation of vegetable life. The vegetable kingdom is created by the world of elements, including soil, water, and air. Elements come into being through the combination of electrons, protons, and other preatomic particles, which are, in turn, condensations of energy. The world of energy or, you may say, vibrations is generated by the primary poles, yin and yang, or centripetal and centrifugal force, that arise within the absolute world of infinity or God.

There are no concrete borderlines between these levels of existence. Each world is one orbit of a single, continuous spiral of change. For example, your body is a continuation of the vegetable kingdom. Every day, you take in vegetable life, either directly or indirectly, and transform it into the cells of your body. These vegetables, furthermore, before you eat them, continually absorb water, minerals, and carbon dioxide, constantly changing these elements into their own vegetable cells.

Likewise, the elements of nature are constantly being formed by the activities of positively and negatively charged preatomic particles, such as protons and electrons, which in turn nourish themselves constantly with vibrations coming to the Earth from throughout the universe. This eternal process of transformation is going on, without pause, at each moment.

Human beings are the last, most materialized stage in this process. We are thus the heirs to the infinite universe. From infinite to infinitesimal, unmanifest to manifest, universal to individual, we gradually emerge, passing through each of these stages of existence. This is our universal origin.

However, when we arrive at the center of this huge spiral of materialization, the force from infinity doesn't stop. It continues to come, and creates us constantly; and because of this vast current, we cannot stop and so begin to go in the other direction. The life current now changes into an outward, expanding spiral that eventually returns us to infinity. When we are in the infinite state, there are no manifestations, no individuality, no differences. There is no you and I, no man and woman, no heaven and Earth. But as we go back toward the center of the spiral again, we start to differentiate once more and take on individual forms; thousands, millions, billions of different forms appear.

Then, as we begin our journey back to infinity, all those divisions and differences slowly dissolve again and eventually merge into one. The first course is one of materialization and the second is one of dematerialization or spiritualization.

The central point of this entire process occurs at the fusion of egg and sperm at the moment of conception. There, deep within the mother's body, at the most inner depths of the universe, our entire voyage from infinity concludes in the form of the fertilized egg. That point is the beginning of our journey back to infinity, which we call the process of growth.

As soon as it is fertilized, the egg begins to spin with great electromagnetic force around its axis, acting as a replica of the larger environment, the Earth. Like tiny mountain ranges, meridians of energy begin to form, and periodic shifts of the rotational axis shape the development of the egg's meridians, organs, and consciousness, just as repeated axis shifts helped mold the geological formation of the Earth. This first, formative stage of growth can be called the first stage of Earth life. From this stage, we then come out to the next, more outer world, passing through the Fallopian tube into the watery environment of the womb. We spend this embryonic period as water life.

Then, when the time comes, after we have sufficiently matured, we come further out, to the next world. Here, on the surface of the Earth, we exist within the Earth's atmosphere as air life. This world is very different from our previous, watery environment, and our functioning here is also different. For example, we now begin to use our lungs, and our sense organs grow much more acute. Therefore, our perception is naturally also very different. Because of this, we easily forget our time as water life, and we cannot easily conceive of it as having been an actual experience while we are living here as air life. It is often a shock to see a newborn baby and to realize that we, too, passed through this stage of life.

From the air world, we then go further out again. Our next environment is the world of vibrations, through which we pass as vibrational life. Since this stage is still in our future and is again very different from our present world, many of us do not have a clear vision of it. Although we talk about the astral or spiritual world, and speak of ghosts and spirits, many of us do not really know what that world is like. Practically everyone has been there before, but again, most of us lost our memory of it when we re-entered the different functionings of Earth, water, and air life forms.

NOURISHMENT AND GROWTH

During our period of water life, our body consists of two parts: one, the placenta, and two, the body itself, which we call the embryo or fetus. These two parts are connected by an umbilical cord. Each part is governed by a different process of growth. During the first part of pregnancy, the placenta grows very actively, but its growth soon stops. The embryo is very small in the beginning, but it continues to grow throughout the pregnancy until it is fully matured and ready to be born into the world of air.

These two patterns of growth perform the different functions of nourishing the body during its water life and preparing it to enter its next life. During pregnancy, the placenta's function is solely to nourish the embryo, while the embryo slowly develops for the purpose of carrying the person's spirit into the next world. These two functions are not actually separate: the quality of the placenta determines the quality of the embryo, which affects the embryo's ability to adapt to the next world when it finally emerges. At the time of delivery, the embryo comes out into the air, followed soon by the placenta. But since its work is now finished, the placenta is separated from the embryo and discarded, while the embryo (baby) continues to grow.

All this is repeated in the next stage. When we are born, we are again differentiated into two parts: one, the body, and two, the head. During the first part of our air life, the body grows actively, but it stops growing when we reach twenty years of age or so. Our consciousness, however, represented by the head, starts out very small and undeveloped, but continues to grow throughout our air life. Or, you may say, our spirituality continues to develop, or our consciousness becomes higher.

Throughout this period, our body is nourished by its outer environment, the Earth, just as our mother's blood nourished the placenta. And the body's primary function is to nourish the growth and quality of the developing consciousness.

This is the key point: the quality of the nourishment our body takes in determines the quality of our mind and spirituality. Many people overlook this point because they don't recognize the unity of body and spirit.

Originally, all great religious and spiritual leaders understood this connection and taught about the importance of food in spiritual development. Moses, Jesus, and Buddha, for example, all practiced and taught a very simple way of eating based on the staff of life: whole grains, fresh local vegetables, beans, and other basic natural staples. In fact, Buddhist and Taoist monasteries in the Orient still serve traditional vegetarian meals. The style of cooking at these monasteries is known as *shojin-ryori*, or "cuisine for spiritual development." It is based on the use of such whole natural foods as brown rice and other cereal grains; processed soybean foods, such as miso, tofu, and soy sauce; fresh garden vegetables; and sea vegetables. Interestingly, the monks who follow this way of eating have also been noted for their longevity and freedom from degenerative diseases.

Many people are surprised to hear that what they eat is the most important factor in their spiritual development. It is so easy to see how this principle operates in embryonic life: if the mother eats the wrong food while she is pregnant—for example, consuming drugs or alcohol—her baby may be physically or mentally handicapped when it emerges into the air world. Even though no trouble may have been apparent while the wrong eating was going on, the new environment creates a challenge to which the baby cannot smoothly adapt. Similarly, the way we eat has a crucial influence on the development of our consciousness and thus on the quality of the life we experience in the next world.

BIRTH INTO THE SPIRITUAL WORLD

When our consciousness is fully matured, we are born into the world of vibrations to exist as vibrational life. The air world is millions of times bigger than the previous water world—as air life, we can travel freely anywhere on the Earth as long as air is there. The vibrational world is again billions of times bigger than the air world.

All biological life separates into two parts at death. One part, the physical body, returns to the Earth. Like the placenta, its primary function is to nourish the development of the other part; when the other part has fully developed and can exist on its own, the physical body is no longer needed. The other part, which we can refer to as the energy body, or consciousness, rises. That part continues to live and can also be called the soul or astral body. In the Orient, the name for the next world is *Yu-kai*. *Yu* means astral, ghost, or soul; and *kai* refers to sphere or world. The physical world is called *Gen-kai*. *Gen* means present, visible, sensory, or detectable. The Gen-kai deals basically with the five senses, while the Yu-kai consists of vibrations that cannot be perceived with our physical senses. Our body in the next world is an energy mass and is called *yu-tai,* or astral body. The body in the Gen-kai is known as the *niku-tai,* or physical body.

The physical world is composed of very condensed vibrations and is a thick form of energy or spirit. In the next world, where energy is more yin or diffused, our lifespan is longer than on Earth. We live about 80 years in this life. In the next world, the Yu-kai, we live much longer. The average is about 600 to 1,000 Earth years. The general ratio is 1 Earth year to 7 years in the spiritual world.

While on Earth, we may be aware of the spiritual world, but it seems vague. When in the spiritual world, we perceive the physical existence, but again only in a general way. In the next world, although conditions are very different, we are still living, still have life. The relation between the physical and spiritual worlds is front and back, antagonistic and complementary. In the Yu-kai, we meet the people we knew in this life; our parents, ancestors, and friends appear in their astral form. Of course, relationships are very different there because we no longer have a physical body.

This new world is divided into two parts: an inner region and an outer region. The inner region is the vibrational sphere of the Earth. As the Earth rotates, it sends off energy that collides with energy coming in from the outer part of the solar system, creating a sphere of intensively charged vibrations. Meanwhile, the Earth's course around the Sun causes this sphere to elongate out behind the Earth like a tail, and the direct influence of the Sun in the form of the solar wind pushes this tail out in a slight curve. Modern science is aware of this electromagnetic field and refers to it as the Earth's magnetosphere.

The Earth's vibrational sphere, however, extends only partially into the spiritual world. The outer region is composed of the entire solar system. It encompasses the Sun and the planets, including the empty space in between each planet, which is also vibrating, and extends into the cometery field, which is many times larger than the planetary field. It moves in a huge spiral motion. The vibrational sphere of the solar system takes on the appearance of a ball. The visible, physical part is the core.

It is covered by the invisible, vibrational field, or aura, of the solar system. Together, they form a complementary, antagonistic unit.

The next solar system, Alpha Centauri, comprises another unit of physical and vibrational energy. This unit is the Yu-kai of that particular system. If our consciousness is refined and fully matured at death, we freely and naturally enter into the next world, initially into the more immediate vibrational sphere surrounding the Earth. Then, as time passes, we go on to the wider vibrational sphere of the entire solar system, traveling freely throughout this immense region.

As we saw in Chapter 2, our physical body, or niku-tai, is charged with the energies of heaven and Earth. We can consider it to be a condensed form of energy and therefore a spiritual entity. Charging our physical body is the invisible energy system that includes the primary channel and chakras. The meridians radiate outward from this central core and, in turn, subdivide into smaller and smaller branches, which ultimately connect with, and charge, each of the body's cells. This invisible structure cannot be detected anatomically and is therefore overlooked by modern science and medicine. However, in ancient times, it was often referred to as the body's spiritual structure. And since it has roots, a main trunk, branches, and leaves, it was also referred to as the tree of life. The roots of this spiritual tree are in the head, centered around the mid-brain chakra. The primary channel is the stem; the meridians are the branches; and the body's cells are the leaves. This invisible body carries, in the form of energy waves, all of the impressions, memories, emotions, and thoughts that make up our individual consciousness. At the time of death, this invisible form separates from the physical body and enters the world of vibrations.

Our life experiences also influence the development of our consciousness. Upon reaching old age—after many successes and failures, joys and sorrows, and difficulties and pleasures—we gradually lose our attachment to the material things of this world. The experiences of life produce a fullness of consciousness, or the sense of having lived a full life. Then, if our condition is healthy as the result of eating well and keeping active, our mind becomes very peaceful and elevated. We start to see past this life and into the universe beyond. As our attachment to this world becomes less and less, we become more and more ready to be born into the next world.

The way we enter the next world is the opposite of the way we enter this one. When we are born into this world, our head assumes a downward position and emerges before the rest of our body. When we are born into the next world, our energy body gathers toward the head and separates from our physical body in an upward direction. At birth, our first breath is an out-breath, the so-called first cry of the newborn. At death, the emphasis is on breathing in. However, we don't breathe downward toward the lungs, but upward toward the top of the head. This more-yin form of breathing accelerates the separation of our consciousness from our physical body.

At the time of death, the life energy that nourished and illuminated each cell is withdrawn into the meridians. Without life energy, each cell soon stops functioning. Then, the energy flowing along the meridians gathers toward the primary channel and chakras. The flow of energy in each of the meridians eventually stops. The chakras then stop charging as energy from the lower body recedes toward the uppermost chakras. The life energy leaves the body from the back of the head, moving in an upward direction.

Finally, the person's astral body detaches from his physical body and begins to float above it. The person has, as the old English expression puts it, "given up the ghost." Once the astral body is free, the person is able to look down on his body from the outside. He may see himself lying in a bed, surrounded by relatives and friends, and may wish to communicate with the people in the room to tell them that everything is all right. However, because the other people are still living within the realm of the five senses, they cannot see or detect the "dead" person's astral body. His new body is not composed of matter, but of vibrations. Aside from being invisible, it is also very flexible, like the morning mist on the mountains. If a "living" person tries to touch it, his hand will pass right through it.

Initially, the astral body is connected to the physical body like a kite on a string. This astral vibrational string can extend for thousands of miles. But, just as the umbilical cord is cut at birth, the astral cord is severed at death. The physical body is the placenta for the vibrational body, and the string connecting the two exists in the physical body as the meridians of ki or electromagnetic energy. If the room in which the person dies is dark and heavy, the connection is maintained for a long time. If the atmosphere in the room is bright, the astral body soon detaches and floats freely. The person then begins to see things such as his house, family members, and immediate neighborhood. He is also met by one or two spirit guides. Like midwives who assist at a natural birth, these spirits appear after death to help with the transition into the next world.

As long as the astral body is attached to the physical body, the person may not know whether or not he is still alive; in other words, he may not know whether he is living as a human being in the air world or has entered the world of spirit. Once his astral body detaches completely, the person gradually realizes that he is no longer living on the Earth, but has started to live in a new dimension in which he will not be nourished by food, air, and water, but by vibrations. One of the earliest impressions a person has in that world is of a dark red light pulsating beneath his astral body. That is the energy field coming from the center of the Earth. Above him, the person also detects a bright, radiating light, toward which he eventually goes.

In our mother's womb, we live in a world of darkness. On the Earth, we live in a world alternating between light and darkness. However, the next world is a world of brightness. An electron is a small, preatomic particle. Vibrations are not composed of matter and take the form of a particle and a wave. We can call them lifetrons, universons, cosmons, or cosmic building blocks. These lifetrons make up the vibrational world. They sparkle and are charged with beautiful light, and the shimmering, radiating world they compose is our home after death.

As we adjust to the astral realm, or Yu-kai, we gain the ability to travel freely throughout the huge dimension of space that it encompasses. Unlike this world, where we have to work hard to actualize our dreams, the vibrational world lets our thoughts immediately become our reality. For example, as soon as we think, "I would like to see a certain person," the image of that person appears in front of us in vibrational form. The thought forms that we carry with us or create in that world are instantly transformed into an experience.

Natural death is a process of spiritual evolution. It is one step in our return journey to infinity, which is our origin, and is simply a transition from this world to the next, just as our birth as a human being is a transition from water to air life. Everyone who is born into this world must die and be reborn into the next. Regardless of who we are or what we accomplish, we all move on eventually. Through dying, we evolve from one dimension to the next. Death is nothing to fear, and when it occurs peacefully after a long and healthy life, it is a natural and spiritually enlightening experience.

RETURN TO INFINITY

Other dimensions of the spiritual world exist beyond the vibrational realm, or Yu-kai. The next world is again billions of times larger than the vibrational world. After a lifetime of 600 to 1,000 years in the astral world, we proceed to the next life, discarding our vibrational body, changing into waves, and being born into the next dimension. In the Orient, this level of life is called *Rei-kai*, or "spiritual sphere," and our body on this level is called *rei-tai*, although it is more like an image than a body as we know it.

This next level of life encompasses the entire Milky Way galaxy, including the huge galactic corona and its invisible vibrating world, which is much larger than the actual galaxy itself. As our vibrational body dissolves and we enter into the galactic world, we ourselves change into rays and waves, and begin to travel at tremendous speeds through vast dimensions. Our consciousness exists in the form of images and thoughts.

In the galactic spiritual world, we are able to materialize on any system within the galactic field. As we saw in Chapter 1, there are about 100 billion solar systems in the Milky Way, each with at least several planets. Many of these planets can support human life. Initially, we manifest in an astral form in our desired system or planet. Then we materialize into biological life and are ultimately born as a human being.

In the galactic world, we can easily make thought into reality. If we think that we want to be born in this particular solar system, on the third planet, as a human being—if we have an image of this—at that moment, we start to materialize on the Earth as a human being. From the perspective of the Earth, however, this process takes billions of years to unfold because the perception of time is so different.

Images that we create in the galactic world also influence the Earth in the form of vibrations. If, for example, we generate positive images of health and peace, these images travel in the form of high speed vibrations to many planets throughout the galaxy. The people who live on those planets receive these impulses through their nervous system and begin to think similar thoughts of health and peace. This can be done on one planet or many, and the people living on the planets receive the image the same way an antenna picks up a radio signal. Often, just a very few individuals among each of the populations are healthy and sensitive enough to pick up and interpret these vibrations. These people begin to teach and act as so-called "messengers of God." Many great spiritual leaders were examples of this.

As we leave the galactic sphere, our territory enlarges again, this time to include the entire universe. This dimension of the spiritual world was traditionally known as the *Shin-kai*, or "sphere of God." In this dimension, our body also changes again, from rays or waves, thoughts or images, into infinite movement at infinite speed. Our waving body eventually becomes a straight line with constantly increasing speed, until we are traveling at infinite speed and reach our final destination, our original home in the infinite world. At this time, our consciousness extends through every dimension of the universe, and we merge with and become infinity itself. Time and space no longer exist for us. We are undifferentiated. We have realized our true self, our origin and destiny.

Our subjective experience of this process begins with the development of a new set of senses in the Yu-kai, or Earth's spiritual sphere. Soon after entering that realm, we begin to see new scenery—including mountains, sky, villages, and people—and for a while, we live within these vibrational surroundings. The images that we see and experience during this stage in our spiritual journey are not actually real, but are images that we ourselves create.

These images change as we proceed to the higher levels of the spiritual world. For example, the dark red light emanating from the center of the Earth gradually disappears and is replaced by a bright purplish-white light, which radiates in all directions. Gradually, we sense that we are living with many other highly evolved spirits, who are something like angels. We may still see faded scenes of mountains, villages, and other scenery from time to time, but these represent our memory of life on Earth. Meanwhile, our life becomes happier and happier as we freely create beautiful images, live with and enjoy them, and dissolve them at will. As we pass into the outer realms of the galactic spiritual sphere and into the universe at large, these images ultimately dissolve completely and change into a bright white light. Our consciousness then radiates throughout the universe in all directions and ultimately merges with the infinite.

It is at this level that we begin the process of taking physical form, first into an image in a particular galactic sphere, then into a solar system's Yu-kai within that galaxy. Next, we condense into our chosen planet's vibrational sphere, and finally, we materialize on the planet. This process comprises the spiral of materialization, or physicalization. If our development proceeds smoothly, we then pass through the following stages: our mother's womb; the air world; the Earth's Yu-kai (the astral or vibrational world) and its various levels; the solar system's spiritual world; the galactic spiritual world; and ultimately, infinity itself.

From there, if you wish, you can freely go back to any universe, any galaxy, any solar system, any planet, and by your free will manifest yourself. This process is known as universal reincarnation and is taking place right now, at every moment. In Genesis, it says that God created this Earth and its life, which conveys the feeling that this event occurred a long time ago. Instead, this is a constant process; creation is going on all the time, right now, every instant. Through the process of universal reincarnation, the unmanifested one manifests into the many, and these many again become unmanifest in an endless cycle.

The cycle of universal reincarnation is an expression of the will of infinity itself. This universal will appears in the galactic radiational sphere as image or dream. Then, in the solar vibrational sphere, it appears as individual spirit, soul, or, you may say, as thought or idea. Here in the physical world, it manifests in the form of individual action and expression.

All of these forms are present within each human being. But as we go toward universal oneness, we gradually dissolve these different forms of will. Here, physical actions are our principal form of expressing will; when we dissolve our body, this too dissolves, and thought and idea become our principal expressions of will. In the galactic world, will expresses itself as the dreams or images that we create, and ultimately, even these dissolve and we merge with the universal current of infinity itself.

GHOST STORIES

From the ghost of Hamlet's father in *Hamlet* to Lincoln's ghost walking at night in the corridors of the White House, ghost stories are found in every culture. Even though science cannot determine whether or not ghosts exist, many people believe in them or have encountered them. Before we discuss whether or not ghosts are real or where they come from, let us first consider the following personal accounts.

After the Second World War, George Ohsawa left Japan to teach macrobiotics throughout the world. His first stop was India, and he and Mrs. Ohsawa traveled there on an ocean voyage that took many days. One night, while his ship was crossing the South China Sea, Mr. Ohsawa was in his cabin reading and writing until the early morning hours. He thought about the many naval battles that had taken place in the area during the war and about the many lives that had been lost. He went up on deck and thought about the cause of war and about his vision of world peace. Suddenly, as if from nowhere, the spirits of hundreds of sailors who had died in the war began to emerge from the waves. They came up to the side of the ship and started tapping on it. The ship came to a sudden stop. They continued tapping for about ten minutes, during which time the boat remained motionless. Then, the spirits returned to the dark ocean and disappeared below the waves, at which point the ship started moving again. No one else had heard the tapping or had seen the spirits, so the reason why the ship came to a stop remained a mystery.

A similar encounter occurred not long ago when one of our associate teachers traveled to Germany to present some macrobiotic seminars. He stayed at an old inn in a small village not far from the Swiss border. Late one night, while half asleep in his dark room, he saw a vision in which people were trying to escape. They were hiding on old-fashioned trains and trolleys, and were very frightened. Along with the vision, our teacher had an actual feeling of fear and pressure that made it difficult for him to breathe. He had the feeling that he also was being chased and woke up with his heart beating rapidly.

The next morning, the teacher related this experience to a second member of our staff who was also visiting from another country. Upon hearing the story, the second person turned pale and said, "Last night, I had a nightmare in which I was being chased by a man with a gun!" The two men then asked several local people about the history of the region and found out that during the war, many people who were trying to flee the country had hidden in the area hoping for an opportunity to cross the border into Switzerland. Some escaped, others stayed in hiding until the war ended, and others were caught. The men now understood that they both had been visited by the spirits of unfortunate people who had died while trying to escape. That night, when the men returned to their rooms, they meditated and chanted to console these spirits. The overall feeling became much more peaceful, and neither one had another vision during the rest of his stay.

Several years ago, Aveline and I were traveling by car through Belgium on the way to a lecture. It was late at night and the drive was taking several hours. It was a warm night, so I kept the window slightly open. As we were driving through the countryside, I began to hear people shouting in the distance. I asked the driver to stop and then asked if anyone else was hearing these sounds. Everyone said no. As I rolled the window down further, the shouting became louder. It sounded as if some type of fighting or battle was taking place. The driver told us that we were passing through a region where a major battle had occurred during the First World War. I realized that I was hearing the ghosts of the soldiers who had died in that battle. For them, the fighting hadn't ended with the Treaty of Versailles, but was still continuing in the spiritual world.

Until several generations ago, many people died naturally. They reached old age with a calm, clear mind and without suffering from chronic illness. Many sensed when their time to die was approaching and even visited their relatives and friends to bid them farewell. Then, when the time came, they passed away peacefully, without pain or suffering. There was no apparent cause of death, and other people thought that they had simply died of old age.

People such as this experience a smooth transition to the vibrational world. A peaceful, natural death is analogous to a natural birth in which a baby develops for the full nine months and is born without struggle. Naturally, these people are ready to be born into the next world, and their experience of that world is positive and bright.

Today, peaceful, natural death has become increasingly rare. Most people die unnaturally before their consciousness has matured fully. They are often attached to this life and are not ready to leave it. They may be struggling with a debilitating illness and, like 80 percent of the people in the United States today, die in a hospital rather than at home. They are often in pain or heavily medicated, or have an array of tubes and wires connected to their body. This type of death is analogous to a premature birth. A person who dies because of sickness often has difficulty adapting to his new environment in the vibrational world.

A person with a mature consciousness is able to detach himself from the cares of this world. He knows that this life is but one stage in the never-ending evolution of the spirit and begins to seek the coming world. However, when a person dies prematurely, he usually has a strong desire to remain in this world, but is forced to leave because his body has become sick. He may be strongly attached to his spouse, children, friends, or other aspects of his earthly identity. If these attachments are strong enough, the person's spirit will have difficulty proceeding to the higher realms of the astral world.

Violent death, whether by war, accident, or suicide, also creates problems in the next world. At the moment of death, a person may be in the middle of an action, perhaps driving a car, fighting, or trying to flee. Then a shock or violence strikes, and he is abruptly separated from his physical form. But his consciousness is not ready for this; it is still actively engaged in living. In many cases, the person doesn't even know he has died. Gradually, the shock subsides, and the person begins to perceive his new world. In the interim, however, his experiences can be chaotic.

Since the astral world is the world of image or thought, whatever we think there becomes our reality. So, if we are attached to money or possessions, we create a reality dominated by heavy, material things, which weigh us down and confine us. If we feel hatred toward others, then we ourselves are surrounded by hatred. Or, if we are fighting in a battle and are suddenly killed, the image of that battle travels with us to the vibrational world. We must struggle within the scenes that we create. However, these images do not actually exist in the spiritual world, but are the product of individual thoughts and experiences. Negative images can prevent us from seeing the vibrational world as it really is—radiating with light—and cause us to be confined in darkness and confusion or, you may say, in hell. It is important to remember, however, that hell does not really exist in the next world, or anywhere else in the universe, but is a creation of our own thinking.

If a person has strong attachments at the time of death, his consciousness often floats in the atmosphere close to the Earth. The Earth's atmosphere, or world of air, is within the world of vibration and is the heaviest, densest part of it. These attachments are sometimes so strong that they cause a person's astral form to wander in the air world for several thousand years, seeking an escape from its self-created hell. The many forms of attachment that can confine a person's spirit to the air world include:

- Attachment to a spouse or lover.
- Attachment to children, grandchildren, or other relatives.
- Attachment to guilt.
- Attachment to material things, such as money, possessions, works of art, or property.
- Attachment to fame, reputation, or social standing.
- Attachment to a profession, enterprise, or other personal or social endeavor.
- Attachment to fear.
- Attachment to the memory of a specific event.

Most of the things that concern us in this life are of little importance in the next. The next world is much larger and brighter than this one. However, strong attachments cause us to experience darkness in that world even though we are surrounded by light. Astral forms that remain in the air world are what people usually refer to as "ghosts."

Rather than perceiving ghosts with the five senses, most people feel or intuit their presence, especially their thoughts and emotions. Their thoughts and emotions exist in the form of vibrations, and we detect them through our meridians and chakras rather than through our nervous system. We are particularly sensitive to these influences when our metabolism is calm and quiet, such as during sleep or meditation.

These influences become stronger in a yin environment. During the day, and especially in the morning, the atmosphere is bright and active, or more yang, while it becomes quiet, dark, and more yin at night. Ghosts tend to be more active at night and less active during the day. They also tend to appear on rainy or humid days, rather than on bright, sunny ones, and tend to gather in dark, quiet places, such as graveyards, rather than in active or busy places. Old battlefields also contain many ghosts, which, as we saw, often act as if the battle is still taking place. Old castles, such as the ones that still exist in Europe, often contain ghosts, as do many large old houses. Ghosts are often found in hospitals. Interestingly, Paris, although beautiful and romantic by day, contains many ghosts of people who died by the guillotine, and these become active at night.

Many encounters with ghosts occur in old houses. If someone committed suicide in a particular room or struggled for many months with a terminal illness before dying, his ghost may still be there, especially if the room is more still, humid, or dark than the others in the house. When people enter that room, they often have a strange, chilly feeling or a sense that something is not quite right. If someone stays in that room overnight, he may have a dream in which the deceased person appears. The ghost may tell the story of how he or she died or may re-enact the scene. Or, the ghost may simply stand at the foot of the bed watching the other person sleep. Meanwhile, the person who is seeing the ghost may be unable to move until the ghost disappears.

More-yin environmental conditions cause ghosts to congeal somewhat, similar to the way water vapor condenses into droplets high above the Earth. Some people may be able to see them when this happens. However, everyone's condition, sensitivity, and perception are different, and therefore so is their ability to perceive ghosts. Very few people can actually see them, although many are able to sense their presence. How we perceive them depends on how strongly they are attached to a particular person or thing, the condition of the environment, and how sensitive we are.

Some people are totally unaware of the spiritual world. The primary reason for this is a lack of sensitivity in the chakras and meridians. As we saw in Chapter 2, the body's energy flow is greatly affected by what we eat. Foods also affect the sensitivity of the skin, and this in turn influences the body's energy system. Steak, hamburger, eggs, cheese, chicken, and other types of animal food contain cholesterol and saturated fat that harden the skin and dull our energy receptors. When we eat too much of these extremely contracting foods, our range of perception narrows and tends to be limited to the world of the senses. We often become insensitive to spiritual influences or deny they are real. In addition, foods such as sugar, tropical fruits, chocolate, drugs, and chemicals disperse the body's energy flow and diminish the clarity of our perception. These foods cause our condition to become overexpanded and interfere with our ability to act as a channel for more refined vibrations. On the other hand, whole grains, fresh local vegetables, beans, sea vegetables, and other complex carbohydrate foods promote skin sensitivity and have a calming and centering effect on the body's energy flow that furthers our awareness of the more subtle vibrations, including those of the spiritual world.

Ghosts can influence living people in a number of ways. For example, they can cause someone to experience dark, depressing, or unhappy feelings. They can also influence a person's thoughts and actions. Although fiction, the story of Hamlet is an example of this latter type of influence. According to Shakespeare's story, the ghost of Hamlet's father, the king, wanted to take revenge on his wife and brother. Since the deceased king could no longer act directly in the physical world, he

Seeing Auras
and Vibrations

Every living being has an aura. An aura is created by the radiation of heaven's and Earth's forces, which continually charge it. Inanimate objects also have an aura, or energy field. The Earth's aura, for example, is called the aurora borealis at the North Pole and aurora australis at the South Pole. Our human aura, however, is especially fascinating because it is influenced by what we think, including our memories and aspirations, as well as by what we eat and drink. It is also influenced by the spiritual world.

Altogether, the human aura has seven different layers. The vibrations of the innermost layer are produced by our body heat and metabolism. The vibrations of the outer layers are produced by our day-to-day thinking and consciousness, as well as by our deeper thinking, memories, and attitudes. The outermost layers can include various spirits that are attached to us or are serving as guardian spirits and watching over us.

From the inside to the outside, the colors of these layers go from yang to yin: from red and orange (more yang), to yellow (balanced), and toward blue and purple (more yin). As a whole, the aura will usually appear more orange. However, if someone eats plenty of meat, poultry, eggs, or other animal foods, his metabolism and caloric discharge become very active, causing a deep red color to predominate and the yin or balanced colors to diminish. If a person eats plenty of sugar, chemicals, chocolate, tropical fruits, or drugs, blue and purple begin to dominate and the other colors diminish. Whole grains and vegetables cause a very harmonious yellow color to appear, which we refer to as a "golden aura." When colors at either end of the spectrum predominate in the aura, it is often a sign of physical or mental imbalance. An overall dark shade means that a person may be troubled by negative or depressing thoughts, in addition to suffering from physical imbalance.

Being able to see auras and other spiritual influences also requires a balanced condition. A diet based on whole grains and vegetables helps keep our physical and mental condition balanced and promotes sensitivity to the many vibrational influences that are a part of our life. We also need to retrain our vision in order to see auras and other spiritual influences.

Just as our speech is trained in childhood, our vision is also conditioned by our early experiences and education. Babies have the natural ability to see both objects and the space in between, including the vibrations in this space. This is why babies often smile at "nothing"; when they do this, they may actually be seeing and responding to things in the vibrational world. But when parents hold brightly colored toys in front of the baby and say, "See this, see that," the child gradually focuses on the solid objects and loses the ability to see the vibrations and empty space.

The following practice, which we call "non-focusing" vision, can help us gain back that natural ability to see vibrations:

1. *Hold your hand out in front of you with your index finger pointing upward. Focus your eyes on the fingertip.*

2. *Without changing your focus, quickly move your finger away. You are now looking directly at a point in space, and if you practice this exercise repeatedly, you will gain the ability to unfocus your eyes and see the vibrations your finger leaves behind.*

3. *Try looking at another person. As you watch him, slightly unfocus your eyes as described in step 2 and breathe out. With practice, you will soon develop the vision to see another person's aura and other spiritual influences.*

enlisted the help of his son, Hamlet. As a result of the ghost's influence, Hamlet began to think and act as the instrument of his father's wishes.

Of course, we also receive many positive influences from the spiritual world. For example, when I was sixteen years old and living in Japan, I became very interested in spiritual issues. I visited shrines every morning before school. Although I had no clear idea of what it was I was seeking, I felt strongly attracted to the world of spirit and went to a certain shrine near my home to pray and meditate. One morning, while deep in meditation, a bright golden light enveloped me and filled my consciousness. The entire universe existed as this golden-white light. While I was experiencing this, a concentrated ball of golden-white light came from within the shrine and surrounded me. It merged with my consciousness and became one with it. Then, the light started to recede. My consciousness returned to normal and I stepped down from the shrine. At that point, everything again became light, and I saw the trees, stones, and clouds pulsate with living energy. The first rays of the morning sun appeared above the trees and were absorbed by this golden light. At this moment, I realized that everything is spirit. Then, the light receded completely and I returned home.

Several years later, I discovered that that shrine had been dedicated to two great personalities who had shared a dream of health and peace similar to my own. One was a well-known scholar of the spiritual world and the other was a proponent of natural farming and diet as a means to health. As I started to teach macrobiotics, I came to understand that these great men were helping and guiding me.

Similarly, many other people have also made positive changes in their life after receiving guidance from the spiritual world. Over the years, several people have told me that they were led to macrobiotics by guardian spirits. They had been struggling for many months with an illness and had had a dream in which the spirit of a deceased person appeared and guided them toward the macrobiotic way. As a result, they changed their way of life and overcame their illness.

Our world and the world of spirit are actually one. Life does not end with death, but continues endlessly. We continually interact with the spiritual world, even if we are unaware of it.

When our condition is clear and healthy, it is possible for us to perceive and communicate with spirits. It is even possible to help people in the spiritual world to free themselves from unnecessary attachments or negative thoughts. The principle for helping others in that world is the same as it is in this one. However, the method is slightly different. Helping others in this world requires that we translate our love for them into tangible action. Helping others in the spiritual world requires that we translate our love into invisible thoughts and images. In the rest of this chapter, we will describe several basic methods for helping people in the spiritual world.

LIFE AFTER LIFE

Lafcadio Hearn, the well-known chronicler of Japan, once wrote about a young boy named Katsugoro. The story seems to offer evidence of reincarnation.

According to Hearn's account, when Katsugoro was a young boy, he frequently expressed a strong desire to visit a particular village where he claimed he had lived before. At first, his parents thought his ideas were only childhood fantasies, but he persisted until they agreed to take him to that village. When they arrived there, Katsugoro kept looking at a certain house and eventually ran up to it, shouting, "This is my house. This is where I used to live." An elderly couple came to the front door, and when Katsugoro saw them, he exclaimed, "They are my parents!"

Katsugoro's parents apologized for their son's behavior and explained to the elderly couple why they had come. While they were talking, Katsugoro interrupted and asked to see the stream and persimmon tree behind the house. The old couple looked at each other in astonishment and answered, "Yes, of course you can, but how did you know they were there?" Katsugoro replied that he had been born in that house and had played often in the backyard. The old couple then asked Katsugoro to describe his childhood experiences, which he proceeded to do. Upon hearing Katsugoro recount several episodes, the old couple became pale and said, "Twenty years ago, we had a son who died while still a child. The events that

Spiritual Diagnosis

Among the many types of diagnosis practiced in Oriental medicine, there is one type that is based on seeing the influences exerted by people who have died. In Japanese, it is known as rei-so, *or "spiritual diagnosis." To explain* rei-so *in modern terms, we can interpret the term "spirit" to mean "vibration," "energy," or "consciousness." Among the spiritual influences we receive, one type has to do with the attachments we have to people who were close to us in life but have since died. If you had a special relationship with a parent, relative, or close friend who has now passed away, his or her spirit may be attached to you. Many people are influenced by spirits of this type, as the following story illustrates.*

Several years ago, a desperate young man came to see me for macrobiotic advice. Not only was he in poor health, but he was suffering from mental and emotional problems. He seemed to be surrounded by a dark cloud, and when he entered the room, the atmosphere became heavy and depressing. Both of his parents had died, he said, and his brothers and sisters were either suffering from mental illness or had experienced an untimely death. When I asked about his family background, he told me that his ancestors had been slave traders in colonial America. This had created a strong negative influence that was still being passed on from generation to generation. Karma, the law of cause and effect, or yin and yang, was causing physical and mental sickness among the members of his family. In order to change his condition and clear up this negative karma, he began to eat macrobiotically, especially avoiding animal foods, and to pray and offer his apologies on behalf of his ancestors to the spirits of the people whom they had forced into slavery. After one year, his condition became much better and brighter.

Wandering spirits appear over the shoulders. If they appear over the left shoulder, they are either male spirits, such as a deceased husband, or are among the father's ancestors. When they appear over the right shoulder, they are either female spirits or are among the mother's ancestors. Spirits that are influencing us negatively create darkness in our aura. Positive spirits are generally brighter.

As this story illustrates, our health may depend on whether we can make our spiritual condition clean and clear by pacifying and releasing any attached spirits. Prayer, self-reflection, and changing the quality of our blood, cells, and entire being through a balanced natural diet are necessary to achieve this. Our ability to console unhappy spirits can ultimately extend beyond those directly influencing us to the entire realm of deluded or unhappy entities. Many people have suffered throughout our long history, and modern civilization was built upon the sacrifice and suffering of an untold number of people. In order to create a truly spiritual civilization in the future, our love and compassion must extend not only to the people who are alive on the Earth but also to those in the invisible realms of spirit.

Katsugoro has described fit perfectly the experiences of our departed son."

Then the old couple asked to see Katsugoro's right leg. It seemed their son had had a birthmark on that leg. To their surprise, Katsugoro also had a birthmark in exactly the same location. By this time, everyone was convinced that what Katsugoro was saying was true.

Reincarnation occurs throughout the universe and at every level of life. It is simply another way of describing the endless cycling back and forth between yin and yang. All things are governed by cycles of expansion and contraction. The movement of water is an example. When water evaporates, it expands upward into the atmosphere in the form of invisible water vapor. Then it condenses back again into visible droplets and falls back to Earth. It rises and falls in an endless cycle of expansion and contraction, or upward and downward movement. Similarly, in the Earth's biosphere, elements in the soil, water, and air change into plant life, and when the plants die, they decompose and release these elements back to nature where they are again taken up and used by a new generation of plants in a repeating cycle.

Reincarnation is not limited to the cycles that occur in the natural world, but also takes place between the visible, material world and the invisible world of spirit, as well as between the various levels of the spiritual world. Life is a continual process of coming and going from one world to the next. For example, when a person dies and enters the astral world, if he is still attached to this world, he may be reborn on Earth instead of proceeding further in the spiritual world. However, the degree of attachment that produces reincarnation is not as strong as that which confines someone's consciousness to the air world. Ghosts are very strongly attached to their previous life and are not ready for a new one. They cannot be reborn on Earth until they graduate from the air world and enter the yu-kai.

Children, especially babies, often have the ability to recall past lives. The power of recall is especially strong during infancy before the so-called "soft spot" on the top of the head closes. Babies sometimes recall vivid images of their past lives, but are unable to describe them in words. Once the soft spot closes, a child begins to assume his new identity, and his conscious memory of his past lives fades. This memory is then stored within his subconscious and may occasionally come to the surface.

The memory of past lives sometimes surfaces in the form of natural talents or abilities. Often, people have skills or talents that seem to be inborn. For example, someone may become a skilled carpenter or learn to play the piano without formal study or training. Or, if he does receive training, he rapidly becomes proficient. A natural aptitude is often an example of someone recovering a skill or ability that was acquired in a previous life. It is as if the person already knew how to do something and was simply remembering it.

Also, many people feel strongly attracted to a certain part of the world. Even though they may have never visited a place, they feel as if they know it and actually miss being there. This is similar to the feeling that people have when they immigrate to another country. They often miss their homeland and long to return. These feelings often come from subconscious memories of previous lives. Similar reactions can occur when a person hears a particular foreign language, reads about a certain period of history, or is exposed to the art and culture of another part of the world.

Reincarnation is governed by the same principle of compensation found throughout the universe. Everywhere, yin and yang alternate with one another. When we walk, we put our right leg forward and then our left. We assume a vertical posture during the day and compensate by lying down at night. Daily, we experience cycles of movement and rest. Whatever we do, an opposite condition eventually arises to make balance with it. In our present life, if we eat plenty of meat and animal food for many years, we may get sick or fed up with our diet and become vegetarian. Or, if we are actively engaged in business or in making money in our early life, in our later years we may become disillusioned and want to enter a monastery and practice meditation. These are examples of compensations, or balances, that occur within one lifetime.

The same principle applies from lifetime to lifetime. Edgar Cayce, the so-called "sleeping prophet," frequently alluded to this in the many "life readings" that he gave. When Cayce entered a trance state and offered advice about diet and health, he often made connections between the sicknesses or difficulties experienced in this life and actions that had been taken in past lives. For example, if someone with an injured leg visited Cayce, Cayce would enter a trance and state that in a past life, the visitor had harmed someone else's leg. The injury was simply a form of balance or compensation for past action. However, compensation—which people sometimes refer to as karma—doesn't imply "punishment," but is simply a form of balance between yin and yang.

On the average, the cycle of reincarnation lasts about 700 years. In other words, a person who dies naturally in old age stays in the astral world for about 700 years before returning to Earth. When someone dies unnaturally or prematurely, however, his astral body often stays in the lower realms of the Yu-kai and he reincarnates more rapidly. He may be reborn several years or even several days after death, although in general it takes about forty-nine days to pass from this world into the Yu-kai. People with a high level of spiritual awareness may not reincarnate on Earth at all, but may stay in the astral world and proceed through to the Rei-kai, or galactic spiritual sphere. There, they gain the ability to reincarnate on other planets throughout the galaxy. They themselves decide whether or not they would like to come back to Earth or go to another planet for a particular purpose. If they decide to materialize, they are born on the planet of their choice and live according to their dream. Often, such people become guides or teachers who help many other people develop their spirituality.

DEVELOPING SPIRITUAL AWARENESS

Our spiritual awareness develops quite naturally when we live in harmony with nature. Everyone is actually on a course of spiritual growth—although everyone is proceeding at a differ-ent speed—and will eventually continue the journey in the invisible world. Each stage in this infinite journey is a prepara-tion for the next. Below, I outline several practical steps that can help you in orienting your lifestyle toward the development of spiritual awareness, beginning with the important role of daily food. For more information on these steps, including a more detailed description of the macrobiotic diet and lifestyle as well as cooking suggestions, see my book *The Macrobiotic Way: The Complete Macrobiotic Diet & Exercise Book*.

Managing Daily Food

Throughout life, our food changes; we cannot eat the same way from childhood to old age. On the way to becoming human, we passed through many stages of existence. Now, to make our return journey, we go back through all of these stages, re-expe-riencing and reuniting with each stage in turn by eating in the opposite order from our evolution.

Our lifetime is composed of a series of graduations, going higher and higher, and our eating should reflect these changes.

If our nourishment doesn't proceed this way, then our development slows down or stops.

Once we arrive here as a fertilized ovum, we begin to nourish ourselves with our mother's blood, the essence of the modern animal world. After birth, we graduate from this stage and go further back into our past by taking our mother's milk, which is representative of the ancient sea where life began. After another short time, we have fully re-experienced all the stages of our animal evolution and graduate from our animal-food-eating period.

Of course, it is fine to occasionally eat some white-meat fish and other seafood if our condition and activity warrant it and if it is properly prepared. But if we continue to take too much animal food after we are weaned and grown, or if we regularly eat land-animal food—including dairy food, eggs, poultry, and meat—then we can't graduate from this limited sphere. This is an important reason to stay away from these foods and to eat primarily vegetable-quality foods.

Then we go back to the vegetable stage of evolution. Within the world of vegetables, cereal grains are the latest development and contain all of vegetable history in microcosm. Also the most highly energized of all vegetable foods, they are best suited to carry us back on our spiritual journey. Vegetarians and fruitarians definitely have more spiritual potential than meat eaters, but they still cannot pass further into the higher spiritual worlds unless they begin to eat grains as their principal foods.

By eating grains as our main food, and not grasses, leaves, or other vegetables, we graduate into adult human status. To become more fully developed, however, we need to continue on and embrace the worlds of elements and preatomic particles or, you may say, plasmic energy. This is the reason we discovered how to cook. Through cooking our grains—mingling them with the elements of water and minerals through the use of fire—we are able to represent these two larger worlds within our diet and thus increase our capacity for spiritual development.

Within this general way of eating that we refer to as macrobiotics, there are several points about which we need to be particularly careful. Regarding whole grains, the majority are best eaten in their whole form, rather than as flour. Baked foods, such as cookies and bread, are prepared with intense heat, which causes the flour to become hard. When eaten excessively, they can cause stagnation and hardening in the body, which interferes with spiritual sensitivity. Whole grains themselves are far more energized than are broken grains or flour.

Also, in cooking side dishes, it is important not to use too much oil. Oil is extracted from a source such as sesame seeds or corn; as soon as it is extracted, its quality changes. Oil is not a whole food, nor is it well-balanced in itself. It is best taken in its original form, as a part of a whole food. For example, brown rice contains natural oils, as do oats and wheat, although only a very small percentage. Whole sesame seeds also contain high-quality oil. A small amount of natural, cold-pressed vegetable oil, such as sesame or corn oil, can of course be used in cooking. But if too much is used, our physical condition will become oily and dull, and the more refined spiritual energies will not be able to penetrate. The same is true of nuts and seeds. Nuts are especially high in oil and fat, and are also best eaten in moderate amounts.

Another point of caution concerns the use of salt. Salt and minerals are necessary in our diet to maintain health and develop spirituality. However, commercially refined table salt, which is almost pure sodium chloride, should be replaced with unrefined sea salt, which includes a much larger scope of minerals that we also need. The point of caution is: be careful not to use *too much* salt. Many traditional macrobiotic preparations combine salt with fermentation, such as miso, tamari soy sauce, umeboshi plums, and pickled vegetables. Fermentation is more yin and balances well with salt, making these foods easier to eat than plain salt. Umeboshi plums, for example, are very interesting—although they are very salty, they also have the very strong sour taste of unripe plums. So, their overall effect is more balanced and they don't create strong cravings or thirst. Many macrobiotic condiments, such as gomashio and sesame-seed–sea-vegetable powders, also combine salt with seeds, making both ingredients more balanced and better for everyday use.

Through these general dietary guidelines, we can attain maximum flexibility and spiritual freedom. There are, however, still two further graduations that we must make as we become a fully matured adult; even until we die, our diet will still develop and change.

Having now reached the preatomic stage, we begin to leave the physical world in our return journey to infinity. Continuing on, we must now reunite with the larger worlds of vibrations, waves, and polarized pure energy, or yin and yang.

Our nourishment takes two different forms during our lifetime: the universal forms of early and mature life, or particle form and wave form. As nourishment for growing children, food can be considered in terms of its physical components, such as minerals, carbohydrates, and proteins. We can refer to the physical aspects of food as the particle form of nourishment. Modern nutrition, which is based on biochemical analysis, can be adapted to understand food during this time of life. Once the body is grown, however, it begins to function more as a placenta to nourish our growing consciousness. At that time, the particle view of food becomes obsolete, and we must graduate to considering food in its wave form. Modern nutritional theories cannot explain this energetic or, you may say, spiritual aspect of food.

As adult nourishment, food must be viewed according to its vibrational quality; it must be seen in terms of, for example, what kind of ki created it, how it influences the flow of energy in the body, and how it affects our consciousness and spirituality. This was the orientation of the medical systems of the ancient Indians, Chinese, American Indians, and other traditional cultures. In order to develop spiritual awareness, we must become sensitive to this wave quality of food.

Once we begin to guide our eating by food's vibrational quality, we gradually become more and more sensitive to the world of spirit. We begin to reunite with the world of polarized energy and eat according to an intuitive awareness of yin and yang balance. As we continue to strive for this understanding, our sense of yin and yang in our food deepens and deepens, and we approach true mastery of our food and of the whole physical world.

Many spiritual teachers advise eating less as a way to accelerate spiritual development. George Ohsawa recommended chewing well—at least until each mouthful becomes liquid—as a way to avoid overeating and to discover how much food is actually needed. As you continue your development as an adult, you can begin to eat fewer side dishes and more grain dishes, along with a smaller volume of food altogether. This is because you are beginning to take less nourishment from your actual food and more nourishment from the non-physical world of vibrations. For just three days, try eating only two small meals a day, with over half of each meal consisting of grains—and chewing very well—and you will see how acute your perception of vibrations can become. At the spiritual training seminars that we conduct at our mountain retreat in the Berkshires, we observe these dietary practices for several days. People who have attended these seminars notice an increased sensitivity to the vibrational world even after just several meals. After death, of course, the need for physical food ceases entirely, and you will be nourished by vibrations alone. But here, in this lifetime, it is important to master the world of physical nourishment and to constantly increase your capacity for vibrations, through thinking, reflection, study, and experience.

Clearing the Spiritual Channel

In addition to attention to diet, there are two other practices I would like to recommend to you. For many of you, due to your past eating habits, or perhaps your present eating habits, you may have stagnation along your spiritual channel, the central or primary meridian of energy that flows up and down the inside of your body just in front of your spine. When you are in good condition, heaven's and Earth's forces are constantly charging this channel; and this charge is distributed throughout your body, creating the rhythms of your cardiac muscles, the peristaltic action of your intestines, the high-speed firing of your nerve impulses, the patterns of your speech, and all the other movements of your daily life. This is not a steady stream of energy, but an alternating current, flowing straight through your body and connecting you directly with the heavens and the Earth in one unbroken, pulsating rhythm.

When your spiritual channel is clear, you automatically feel at one with the environment, physically, mentally, and spiritually. When the channel is blocked, however, something resembling a constipated condition arises; the energy can't alternate smoothly, and your organs, nerves, and mentality are all affected. Not being able to express yourself in words is an example. In addition, this condition is what helps fear develop: as you are cut off from the vibrations around you, you begin to feel isolated and alone. The entire universe, including the world of spirit, is there for you to experience and enjoy, only you don't know it; you can't feel it.

This condition, which we call spiritual stagnation, produces a variety of symptoms, including arrogance, schizophrenia, stubbornness, narrow-mindedness, fear, prejudice, emotional upset, anger, irregular heartbeat, rapid breathing, sexual weakness, and uncontrollable talking and laughter. If you have any of these symptoms, or if you can't make decisions quickly or be friendly to everyone you meet, you are already suffering from this stagnated condition.

What creates this unhappy condition? The main cause is an unbalanced diet, with too much animal food (especially animal fat and dairy foods), oily or greasy dishes, flour products, sugar, icy cold foods and drinks, and sometimes excessive salt. Also, overeating in general, together with laziness and lack of activity, contributes to blockage along the spiritual channel.

All traditional exercises, disciplines, and spiritual practices were aimed directly at dissolving this stagnation. Special breathing, dancing and movement, and chanting can all be used to direct your ki to certain chakras to help disperse the blocked energy there. Together with eating well, the following two simple practices can also be used to help this condition. The first is simply to be active physically, mentally, and spiritually. Anything is fine—studying, scrubbing floors, working hard at a job—it doesn't matter what. You should just take care to be regularly active in all three ways; don't be one-sided or you will favor one chakra over another, one way of thinking over another, one type of eating over another, and will fail to achieve overall harmony or balance in the flow of energy throughout your body and mind.

The second practice is a very simple chant. The sound *AAA* (pronounced *AHH*) vibrates in the body's lower region (intestines and stomach); the sound *UUU* vibrates in the body's middle region (heart and lungs); and the sound *MMM* vibrates in the upper region (throat and head). When you make these sounds together, *A-U-M*, repeating them perhaps twenty times every day, you will be able to easily clear your entire spiritual channel of blockage and stagnation. Sit in a relaxed position with your spine very straight. Close your eyes and let your mind quiet down. Then breathe in and make the sound *A-U-M*, long and slow, with deep breaths. After you finish, remain silent for about one minute. Then clap your hands sharply twice and resume your activities.

Dispelling Illusions

When you eat well and keep active and busy, your body nourishes your consciousness properly, and you perceive true thoughts, true dreams, true images—in other words, reality. But if you feed your body inappropriate types or amounts of food, your consciousness is also improperly nourished, and it can't function well. Your perception is filtered and distorted, and you see illusions and build up a world of delusion in your thinking. Living within this false image of the world, you grow accustomed to it and become a slave to your delusions.

There are two types of delusions to clear up. The first is delusion of memory. The front part of the brain is involved more in future-thinking, dreams, and aspirations, and the back part is used more for past-thinking and memory. If you eat more vegetables, salads, and fruits, the front part of your brain is more stimulated, creating more future-thinking. If you eat more animal foods and salt, the back part of your brain is more stimulated and your past-thinking is stronger.

If you are attached to or bothered by a dark or unhappy memory, you must first change the food that is stimulating that kind of thinking; if you eat animal food, dairy food, or fatty, greasy food, you cannot forget. You may be carrying a bitter memory of an unhappy experience from childhood, and this may be creating deep anger, guilt, or complexes. However, it is not your unhappy experience that is creating your present misery, but rather your memory of it and your present way of seeing it that are holding you down, supported by your biological condition. Freud was a very intelligent, interesting man, but he never discovered that psychological problems are simply the natural result of a heavy, sticky diet, which produces a heavy, sticky consciousness.

You can accelerate the discharge of a dark memory by changing your view of it. A memory such as this is subjective—you are the one who has been suffering. Now, to detach from that memory, make the experience more objective; in other words, make it clear in your mind and view it from outside yourself. If you are a more extroverted type, it may be easier to do this by talking; speak up and tell someone about the experience. As you formulate a more objective image of it so that you can describe it clearly, its quality changes and you can let go of it more easily.

Another way, if you are hesitant to talk about it, is to write about the experience, in clear, objective sentences. Then you can extend your thanks for the bitter experience, for example by thinking that it helped you learn so much about life, including how foolish we often are. Make your memory more objective, learn from it, express your appreciation for it, and then let it go.

The other type of delusion is present delusional thinking. This is difficult to change because we are often too involved in it to see it clearly. Also, society tends to reinforce these delusions. For example, many people today believe that animal protein is superior to vegetable protein and that large amounts of animal food are necessary for good health. Although some white-meat fish and other forms of seafood can be eaten in a temperate climate to supplement a grain-and-vegetable-based diet, the current over-reliance on meat, eggs, chicken, and dairy foods is a major cause of the modern epidemic of heart disease, cancer, and other degenerative illnesses. Besides, this way of eating has contributed to the widespread disruption of the environment and the uneven distribution of essential resources. For example, the production of animal foods is responsible for generating over half of the pollution burden entering the nation's lakes and streams. It is also responsible for the widespread loss of soil productivity through erosion and mineral depletion, as well as for the continuing destruction of the Earth's tropical rain forests. Moreover, 90 percent of our grains and legumes and approximately one half of our fish catch are fed to livestock, while 800 million people are going hungry.

International politics is also based on an illusory view of reality. When I was young, I looked forward to my first plane trip with great anticipation. I had studied many maps in school and was very excited about the idea of seeing those vast borderlines between the various states and countries, and the huge stretches of green, red, yellow, and blue. When my first plane trip was finally underway, I looked out the window and was very surprised. There are no borders at all; only forests, rivers, oceans, and mountains. The maps I had studied were totally imaginary.

Millions of people act as if modern nations really exist—they carry passports, talk about citizenship, and so forth. However, this is nothing but a conception that somebody made up. No such thing exists, actually—it is an untrue, unreal world. Nature did not create this; the rains, wind, clouds, and air are free to travel wherever they like. If one country's industry spoils its part of an ocean, this destruction doesn't have to stop at any border to be checked before it can proceed. It spreads freely wherever the currents take it. Yet we have divided the whole world into sections, with different ownerships, sovereign rights, taxes, governments, and so forth. It is like a huge children's game—"let's pretend that this is yours and that is mine"—only, 99 percent of humanity totally believes the game and lives within it, spending trillions of dollars and even killing each other to preserve it.

It is important for each of us to wake up from our delusional world, to understand who we are and what life really is, and to see clearly our origin and destiny within the vast order of the universe. It is up to us whether we live in hell or paradise after death, within a heavy mass of delusions or within the huge radiating world of light. Hell does not exist as a punishment for what we did in this life. Hell is our own creation, something we make ourselves within our own delusions. If we eat badly and go to sleep at night, we often see nightmares. We struggle, but we cannot escape until we wake up. This nightmare we created ourself. Hell is created in exactly the same way. The essential point is: we need to wake up from all our delusional hells in this life, so we can pass freely to the infinite world.

To help accomplish this, you can practice a very simple meditation of nothingness. Just sit in a relaxed pose, with a straight spine and empty mind, for five minutes or so. Free your mind of unnecessary thoughts, and breathe naturally and quietly. This meditation helps to clear the mind of delusional thinking by allowing the forces of heaven and Earth to flow freely through the body. Of course, a calm, clear mind is easier to achieve when you are eating a diet based on whole grains, fresh local vegetables, and other complex carbohydrate foods, and are avoiding animal food, sugar, chemical additives, and refined foods.

When we wake up from our delusions, we begin to see the human world as truly ephemeral. We are then similar to a traveler—experiencing and learning many wonderful things as we pass through this life, enjoying all the wonderful scenery. But we have no attachments to anything we do or experience. And when it comes time to leave, we can say to everyone very happily, in words or in the mind, "Goodbye; thank you very much. It is such a wonderful life; please enjoy it a little while longer. I will go ahead now."

As we approach death, even if it is just one hour or five minutes before it, reaching this kind of understanding helps so much to change the quality of our next life. Despite suffering from illness or cloudy thinking, regardless of the stage of our condition, it is important to eat properly, even if only for several days or a week, and to clear up any delusions or attachments that we may have. Eating a naturally balanced diet helps to change our body and vibrational quality and, at the moment of death, allows us to pass through far more peacefully and with less attachment. As a result, our life in the spiritual world is far, far happier.

Communicating With the Spiritual World

An important part of realizing spiritual freedom is to clarify your relationship with any spirits that might be attached to and disturbing you. When you wish to communicate with and help these spirits, first make yourself very quiet and calm, and let yourself become one with the heaven and Earth forces that are passing through you. In other words, become a clear channel or representative of the universe.

Of course, the way you eat has a very real effect both on whether you are able to do this and on the quality of the energy you radiate. For maximum conductivity of the forces of heaven and Earth, it is important to eat a naturally balanced diet that helps dissolve stagnation while maintaining a calm and even metabolism. A macrobiotic diet is ideal for this purpose. Animal foods that contain plenty of saturated fat and cholesterol block the smooth flow of energy in the body and interfere with the conductivity of higher vibrations. Refined sugar, honey, tropical fruits, and other forms of simple sugar tend to scatter the body's energy and make it difficult to quiet and focus the mind.

To empty and purify your spiritual channel, sit with a straight but relaxed posture and chant *A-U-M* several times. Then enter into a meditation of nothingness, making yourself very centered. You can also wipe off all surrounding disorderly vibrations by clapping twice, sharply, before starting your prayer.

You can pray in words or you can just think; the sounds are not important, only the vibrations of your thoughts. So it doesn't matter if you speak or think, or if you do either in English, Russian, or Japanese. The important thing is to have a sincere spirit.

Your prayer can include three elements:

1. Gratitude. If you are communicating with a parent or ancestor, extend your sincere thanks to him for making your life on Earth possible. Your gratitude can also be offered to other spirits as well. You can thank any spirit for his contribution to the world you are now enjoying.

2. Reassurance. Many spirits attach themselves to their children, grandchildren, and other relatives because they are worried about their health and well-being. To help reassure these spirits, extend to them your sincere promise to make yourself healthy and happy, and to distribute these qualities to your family, friends, and many other people.

3. Encouragement. Extend to the spirits your wish for them to freely leave behind this tiny, ephemeral world and to proceed with their endless spiritual journey. Encourage them to become peaceful and happy on their return to infinity.

The time this kind of prayer takes can vary; it may take one minute or ten minutes. After you finish, harmonize yourself with your surroundings, including all the spirits, with the simple, universal sound of *SU* (pronounced like the name Sue). Make this sound several times, using a long, slow out-breath, before you end your session. This is very simple to do, taking altogether just several minutes.

If you are suffering heavily, you can repeat this practice every day. If your suffering is not so heavy, then every week may be enough. Particularly when close relatives and ancestors are involved, however, it is better to do this every day at first, then gradually change to every two days, then every three days, and finally once a week. It may take altogether two or three months to clear up this kind of problem, but afterwards you will definitely be brighter and happier.

You can also improve your communication with the world of spirit by making a simple offering of food along with your prayers. The basic principle is simple. In a quiet space, put a small shelf or table made of wood. You can also place on the shelf a picture of the deceased, or one of his favorite possessions.

All spirits' troubles originally started because they did not eat the proper food when they were in this life. By sending to them the vibrations of good food, you can help them to clear these problems away. The offering can include any balanced, natural food, as long as the food is of vegetable quality; animal food should never be offered to spirits. Ideally, you should take the first portion from your first meal of the day. The minimum necessities are cooked brown rice or another cereal grain, or raw brown rice or another whole cereal grain; sea salt; and clean water. These staples are essential to life. Put the rice or other grain in the center of the shrine and arrange the water, which is more yin, to your left, and the salt, which is more yang, to your right. When you make this offering, you can also pray.

Other members of your family can also offer prayers and consolation. And you can all gather by the shrine whenever there is a special family event to allow your family spirits to share the occasion, whether it is happy or sad. In other words, treat these family members as if they are still alive—they are alive, actually, as thought and spirit. This way of family living

Vibrational Influences

Sometimes I like to drop in to an antique store, but not because I am looking for furniture. I like to feel the vibrations the old objects are carrying and to sense what kind of people used them, what kind of personality and family the owners had, and how they lived and died.

One ornament may have a very happy feeling; it was used by a happy person. Another ornament, when you see or touch it, gives you a strange feeling; the person who used that object was probably unhealthy and living with delusions.

Sometimes you may borrow a friend's clothing to wear. Those clothes have absorbed the vibrations your friend was discharging when he last wore them. So when you put on his clothes, those vibrations go through your meridians and your skin, and affect your health and thinking. Then, you begin to feel the same way your friend was feeling.

When you travel, you may stay in a hotel and sleep in a hotel bed. Even though the sheets have been changed, the blankets, mattress, and bed frame itself still carry the previous occupant's vibrations. Then when you sleep, you may have unusual dreams or may even dream what happened to that person the previous night.

A husband and wife influence each other very deeply through their vibrations. Through talking and touching, and especially through intimate contact, they are constantly exchanging vibrations. If both are eating well, then both are constantly getting better. But if one is eating well and the other is eating poorly, the former's condition will become worse by their exchange of vibrations and the latter's will become better. When you marry, please choose a person who is healthier than you are—then you can easily improve your health.

is not particular to Far Eastern cultures, although it has survived there longer than in the West; originally, this was a common thread found in societies throughout the world.

These simple practices can help everyone develop a greater spiritual awareness. Our life on Earth is but one part of an endless spiritual journey. During the course of that journey, each of us experiences hundreds of lives. We all come from, and eventually return to, the infinite universe. We are all brothers and sisters of one infinity. Therefore, regardless of our differences, let us love and help each other. Each of us is a part of the planetary family of humanity, and we are all proceeding toward the light of the spiritual world on our way back to our infinite home.

In 1956, Mr. Bootman, a bank manager, took a photo of the inside of Eastry Church in England. Although the church was empty when he took the picture, the photo revealed the translucent image of a priest seating in a pew.

The apparition of Raynham Hall in Norfolk, England was captured on film in 1936 by Captain Provand. The ghostly image had been seen by several guests and visitors. The spirit is believed to be that of Dorothy Walpole, a former resident of Raynham Hall.

5.

Predictions for the Twenty-First Century

In the midst of the street of it, and on either side of the river, was there the tree of life, which bare twelve manner of fruits, and yielded her fruit every month: and the leaves of the tree were for the healing of the nations.

Revelation
Chapter 22

As we move through the final decade of the twentieth century, we are at the threshold of an extraordinary period in human history, a time of great difficulties, great challenges, and even greater opportunities. Up until this time, we have of course already encountered many difficult circumstances, but events in this period leading up to the twenty-first century could affect the course of civilization for thousands of years to come. The challenge we are now facing is nothing less than the culmination of our civilization's self-destructive course of development, from the dawn of recorded history up to the present time. Before we consider the possible outcome of this critical time, let us review the natural forces that are playing a decisive role in human events.

Among the many celestial influences being received by the Earth, that of the northern sky is having a profound effect on human history. This influence is not fixed or static, but is slowly changing with the movements of the Earth through space. As the Earth is spinning on its axis and revolving around the Sun, it is also moving in a third much slower cycle, which is sometimes called the procession of the equinoxes. Gyrating like a spinning top, the Earth's polar axis is constantly changing position in relation to the plane of the Milky Way galaxy. Extending the North Pole in a line out to the stars, we can see that this motion is tracing a great circle in the northern sky called the path of the northern elliptic. This cycle is taking about 25,800 years to complete.

During this cycle, the Earth is passing through different stages, with various stars and constellations shifting directly overhead. As a whole, the Earth is surrounded by a vast protective belt of electromagnetic fields, but the area over the North Pole is relatively open. The shower of energy from the particular stars there is therefore exerting a strong influence on the Earth and on human civilization. As they slowly shift position, these stars are producing a regular change in the electromagnetic charge on the Earth in a 25,800-year cycle of historical tendencies.

At present, the star Polaris is almost directly overhead; in the year 2102, it will arrive at a position exactly over the North Pole. This will signal the beginning of the half-cycle, or 12,900-year period, in which the stars of the Milky Way galaxy will come directly over the North Pole.

Humanity last experienced this half-cycle "age of light" from about 24,000 to about 13,000 years ago. During that time, the Earth's axis moved more into line with the plane of the galaxy, and the northern sky was covered with thousands of stars. We were constantly bathed in a shower of light and radiation (so much so that even the deepest nighttime was fairly bright), which poured in through our spines, chakras, meridians, and trillions of cells. We became very highly energized, and our consciousness developed extraordinary insight and powers. At that time, people used more of their brain capacity than they do at present.

Then, about 13,000 years ago, we moved out of the galactic plane as the star Vega of the constellation Lyra came overhead. Our consciousness gradually dimmed, together with the Earth's electromagnetic charge. This was later chronicled as the age of Paradise Lost, for during the previous age of light, humanity had reached tremendous scientific, cultural, and spiritual levels

The Golden Age

Myths and legends from around the world often refer to an ancient "golden age" that predated recorded history and was destroyed in a huge cataclysm. The legend of Atlantis plays an important role in many of these myths. According to Plato, Atlantis was a large continent in the Atlantic with huge fertile plains and an advanced civilization. In two of his dialogues, Timaeus and Critias, *Plato says that this earthly paradise disappeared beneath the sea "in a single day and night." He estimated the date to be 9,000 years before his time, or about 11,500 years ago.*

In his 1931 book, The Lost Continent of Mu, *British investigator James Churchward presents various ancient records that tell of a similar lost civilization, this time in the middle of the Pacific. According to Churchward, the lost continent known as Lemuria or Mu contained a spiritually enlightened civilization and was the center of the ancient world. The legends state that like Atlantis, Mu was struck all at once by earthquakes, volcanoes, and tidal waves, and sunk below the ocean. Churchward estimates that Mu sank between 12,000 and 13,000 years ago.*

Stories of a great flood and the disappearance of a spiritually developed civilization can be found in the written records and oral traditions of Sumeria, Babylonia, Assyria, Persia, and other ancient Mediterranean and Near Eastern cultures. They also exist in ancient Norse mythology, as well as in the mythologies of India, China, and the Maya, Hopi, Aztec, and other tribes of North and South America. The Quiche' Maya, for example, regarded the ancient world as a true paradise where all people lived in harmony. They believed it was destroyed when the god Hurakan (Hurricane) became angry and flooded the Earth. Most of these legends state that the survivors of this global catastrophe struggled for many centuries until they were able to build new civilizations.

and maintained a peaceful worldwide civilization. This ancient civilization then collapsed through a series of natural catastrophes that ushered in the next half-cycle, or "age of darkness."

Legends and mythologies record the destruction of this period. The continents of Atlantis and Mu sank as a result of the natural upheaval. It was a time of drastic changes on the planet, a period of great hardships. To survive these extreme environmental conditions, humanity was forced to widen its diet. The earlier practice of eating grains and vegetables as the primary foods had to be abandoned in certain areas. Other, more extreme foods were included in the diet, each exerting a particular effect on the health and outlook of humanity. The constellation Draco, the Serpent, was clear in the night sky; the ancients thus recorded that paradise was lost by eating forbidden food under the persuasion of the serpent.

During the last 12,000 to 13,000 years, the Earth's energy has continued to steadily decrease. A period of milder climate about 6,000 years ago prompted the Sumerians, Egyptians, ancient Chinese, and various other peoples to again build toward a one-world civilization. The difficult times were passing and mankind spread across the Earth. Various megalithic structures—such as the pyramids, Stonehenge, and other astronomical observation points found around the world—stand as testimony to an awakening consciousness and a growing interest in the mysteries of the universe.

The adversities did not pass quickly, however. Under the influence of the Great Bear and then the Small Bear constellations, war and conflict prevailed. The age of fire was an outgrowth of this period. Built on the power of fire, a materialistic civilization rapidly developed. The overall course of history continued, with the civilizations of humanity struggling in darkness, fighting nature by inventing even bigger and more destructive technologies.

As the influence of Polaris and the Milky Way galaxy began to charge his brain cells about 2,000 years ago, man returned to a predominately vegetable-quality diet. As a consequence, his sensitivity increased, and the coming of a new age, a time of one peaceful world, was foreseen. Before this one peaceful world can be achieved, however, humanity must pass through another crisis and survive the destructive potential of fire technology.

Ancient prophets, such as Buddha and Jesus, warned of this impending time of judgement.

This is the celestial and historical background of our present epochal challenge; our more conventional recorded histories all chronicle the events within this age of decreasing electromagnetic influence—and this period of our history is now drawing to a close. Paradise is clearly approaching. We are living in an historic epoch, with challenges appearing with increasing frequency. At the same time, a reawakening is being experienced, especially among the people who eat whole grains and who are developing a physical and spiritual quality similar to that of the ancient prophets. These people are growing aware of the tremendous potential of the human heritage. Understanding the order of the universe, they are able to transmute the difficulties of our present era into opportunities for growth and development.

THE TURNING POINT

The ancient Oriental calendar divides history into major periods of change, each lasting 120 years. The 1990s are a critical decade, coming at the beginning of the 120-year period of 1982–2102, when Polaris appears directly overhead. This is, in other words, the beginning of the last major period in this large chapter in our history. Our 12,000 years of struggling materialism have now reached their peak; during these final 120 years, as Polaris approaches the position of due north, the institutions of our more analytical, materialistic civilization will pass away, while the next half-cycle's age of light will usher in a new era, dominated by a more holistic, spiritual outlook.

At this critical time, humanity has begun to polarize sharply into two groups: those who are continuing to pursue the concepts of the rapidly passing materialistic epoch and those who are turning ahead to face the future and lay the foundations for the emerging epoch of planetary health and peace.

In general, the events of the next 120 years will bring a gradual decline and the eventual disintegration of the first group, through degenerative disease and the collapse of established institutions and ways of thinking. The second group, meanwhile, will gradually move into the center of society, taking over and transforming the various functions of civilization one by one.

This is the general historical tendency according to the order of the universe. But we cannot make the mistake of thinking that this will all happen automatically. While it may be reassuring to know that a new world governed by peace, harmony, and spirituality will soon arrive, there is no guarantee that this will actually happen. There are several major obstacles that must be overcome for this long-cherished dream of humanity to be realized. At the core of our modern notion of progress, for example, are several self-destructive tendencies that over the centuries have gradually spread and intensified. Today, they have developed such a momentum that if not reversed could lead to the decline, or even extinction, of humanity on this planet. Below we consider the most important of these trends.

The Modern Health Crisis

The modern health crisis is far deeper than the problem of inequality in the distribution of medical technology or the astronomically high cost of high-tech medicine. These are merely surface results of a deep-seated decline in humanity's physical and mental health. Due in part to the gradual loss of traditional ways of eating and the relatively recent introduction of refined, chemicalized, artificial foods and food preparations, this trend has now reached global proportions. The development of modern farm practices, such as the use of synthetic fertilizers, pesticides, and other agricultural chemicals, has contributed greatly to this trend. Through government promotions and commercial advertising, these destructive farming methods have also spread throughout the world, followed everywhere by a rise in chronic diseases.

In the United States, out of a population of about 240 million people, about 43 million suffer from heart and cardiovascular disease; this is nearly 20 percent of the entire population. About 37 million have high blood pressure, and 36 million suffer from allergies. About 32 million—or roughly 15 percent of the population—suffer from arthritis. About 11 million have diabetes, and about 1.8 million have a stroke in this country every year.

Currently, one out of three people in the United States is expected to develop cancer at some point in his life. Forty years ago, the rate was about one out of seven, and at the beginning of the century, it was about one out of twenty-five.

About 25 percent of the population will suffer at some time from some form of mental illness, and about 10 percent of the population will require psychiatric care. A large number of people will eventually be disabled because of mental illness; they will be unable to work or function normally.

Reproductive abilities have also declined in the twentieth century, with infertility now affecting about one out of five American couples. According to one study, average sperm counts have dropped approximately 30 percent over the last sixty years. And estimates are that as many as 20 percent of young men do not have the ability to fertilize an ovum: their sperm counts are either too low, their sperm are too weak, or they are impotent.

Every year, about 700,000 women undergo hysterectomies, so that by the time women reach the age of sixty-five, 50 percent have no ovaries or uterus. In the last few years, herpes and other sexually transmitted diseases (STD) have assumed epidemic proportions; conservative estimates are that 20 to 30 million Americans are now infected with the herpes virus. Moreover, acquired immunodeficiency syndrome (AIDS) is continuing to spread, not only in this country, but around the world. Estimates place the number of people infected with human immunodeficiency virus (HIV) in the United States at between 2 million and 3 million. Some public health officials believe that AIDS will be the world's leading health problem during the remainder of this century and into the next. Clearly, America and the rest of the world is in the middle of a crisis in health that could, if not reversed, lead to the eventual collapse of our modern way of life.

The Threat of Nuclear War

Even though political tensions between the United States and Soviet Union have eased in this era of *glasnost* and *perestroika*, the danger of nuclear war—either by intention, accident, or miscalculation—is still with us. And it will continue to exist as long as humanity possesses nuclear weapons or the knowledge and desire to build them. At the same time, the increasing computerization of defense systems has reduced human participation in the decision-making process that could trigger the end of man on this planet. In one eighteen-month period during the 1980s, for example, the North American Defense Command reported 151 computer failures signalling a Soviet attack. The lead-time prior to a missile launch is from six to ten minutes.

During the 1950s, this country was acutely aware of the dangerous possibility of atomic war. Everyone who lived through that period has memories of air raid drills and other civil defense maneuvers. Recognizing the tremendous scale of destruction that the atomic bomb would wreak in an all-out war, the leading intellectuals of the day began to actively organize an alternative system of world federal government to prevent the possibility of future international war. These people realized that another world war would very likely mean the extinction of the human race. However, the tensions of the Cold War overshadowed the world federalist movement, and today the movement lies dormant.

Today, when the destructive arsenals of the superpowers are far more vast than they were in the fifties, I am constantly amazed to hear Americans speak so nonchalantly about war. Young people often have an unrealistic notion of it, perhaps imagining it to be something like an electronic battle on a video screen. This is not the case in Europe or the Soviet Union, where people are much more aware of its danger and consequences. But many people in the United States are too young or too unrealistic to remember the experience of war or to imagine how truly horrible the reality of nuclear war would be.

In war, you cannot survive unless you kill others, and they cannot survive unless they kill you. So you do your best to murder each other in a very cruel, brutal, and miserable way. On a nuclear scale, this savage exchange would be unthinkably grotesque. Unless you have directly experienced the horror of war, it is impossible to image it.

Despite all our best intentions and sincere desire for non-aggression, until now, worldwide military escalation seems to have been inevitable. During the 1980s, the United States and

Soviet Union each had about 750,000 armed troops stationed abroad. Other countries in Europe, Asia, Africa, and the Middle East had another half million soldiers on foreign soil. The cost of the modern arms race is astronomical. For example, the nations of the world are spending an estimated $800 billion annually on defense and war. By comparison, the United Nations' six largest agencies together are spending per year the equivalent of only one-and-a-half days' worth of the arms race. Fifty percent of the world's engineers and physicists are directly employed in weapons development. In addition to massive nuclear arsenals, estimated to consist of between 50,000 and 60,000 nuclear warheads, the United States and the Soviet Union each have an estimated several hundred tons of deadly poison gas, including nerve gas, stockpiled for military use.

In the early 1980s, when I lectured throughout Europe and the United States, people asked me what I thought the chances were of a nuclear war breaking out in the next ten years. At that time, the Soviets had just invaded Afghanistan and the United States was gearing up for a massive military buildup. I replied that unless the situation changed, the chance of a nuclear war occurring during the 1980s was at least 90 percent. Since then, the movement for nuclear disarmament has grown from a small grassroots effort to a global mandate. The Iron Curtain and Berlin Wall have come down, and the Cold War seems to be ending. Moreover, macrobiotic education is spreading rapidly in Eastern Europe. My associate teachers and I have visited Yugoslavia, Hungary, Czechoslovakia, Poland, and the Soviet Union and have been well-received by doctors, government officials, and the general public. However, in spite of these developments, nuclear weapons still exist, as do massive defense budgets and a high state of military preparedness for war. Moreover, nuclear proliferation has added a new dimension to this crisis. A nuclear war could break out regardless of the intentions of the superpowers. Since World War II, there have been 160 armed conflicts between nations, resulting in 16 million deaths, mostly of civilians. The rate of new wars has increased from an average of nine a year in the 1950s to fourteen a year in the 1980s. As nuclear weapons spread to more countries, the increasing possibility of their being used in a local or regional conflict has altered the character of the atomic threat. Clearly, nuclear weapons pose a massive and continuing threat to humanity on this planet.

Family and Social Decline

This third crisis is more subtle and indirect in comparison with the first two, yet it actually supports and encourages the continuing development of destructive farming, poor food, and military spending.

Present society does not educate its young people in basic human matters, such as how to maintain health and order in daily life. It does not emphasize respect and love for others or teach how to develop harmonious friendships, relationships, families, and other social relations. While ignoring the spiritual nature of humanity, modern education prompts the profit motive in its students, giving them the necessary skills and attitudes to satisfy their quest for money-making. This is done, of course, in the name of a "higher standard of living"for both individuals and society—but how is that standard judged? It is weighed exclusively in material terms, such as how much money is earned; how many car phones, VCRs, and other consumer goods we have; how extensive our stock portfolio is; and how much real estate we have accumulated.

Under the influence of such a materialistic education and the narrow individualistic values it promotes, and already weakened by biological and biochemical degeneration, the modern family is falling apart. Parents are no longer true parents; children are no longer true children; the biological, social, and spiritual identity of the family is no longer passing smoothly from one generation to the next. This has signalled the end of human tradition.

I have spoken recently with many friends who come from broken homes and can see how profoundly it has affected them, how difficult it is to make up for that loss. My advice to people who are thinking of separation or divorce due to difficulties in marriage is to reflect carefully on why you married in the first place and on whether you truly wish for your dream together to end now. This is especially important if you have children. Separation or divorce makes it much more difficult for children to carry their parents' and ancestors' spirit and tradition into the future.

About 200 years ago, thousands of Africans were brought by force to this country to help develop a burgeoning plantation industry. When they arrived in America, husbands were separated from wives, and children from parents; their names were changed and they were sold off to owners from different parts of the country. They were totally cut off from their biological, cultural, and spiritual heritage. They no longer knew their ancestors: who they were, what they had accomplished, where they had lived, or what sort of people they had been. In other words, they lost a large part of the meaning of their lives.

This technique has been repeated countless times throughout history. Separation of tribes, clans, families, and individuals is the most effective way to bring about spiritual, intellectual, and social decay and to create slaves. And today, we are voluntarily doing this to ourselves. At the turn of the century, one in twelve marriages ended in divorce. By 1940, the rate had increased to one in six. In 1970, it was one in three, and in the early 1980s, it was one in two. As a result, more than half of all children under eighteen (13 million) now live in a home with one or both parents missing.

The decline of the family has fueled the modern epidemics of crime and drug abuse, including violence in the schools. In a typical month, 282,000 secondary students are physically attacked; 112,000 are robbed; and 2.4 million are burglarized at school. Meanwhile, 125,000 teachers are threatened with physical assault or violence, and 1,000 teachers require medical attention from actually being attacked while in school. From 1970 to 1980, there was an estimated 50 percent increase in illegal drug use and a 250 percent increase in the use of prescription drugs such as tranquilizers, sedatives, and stimulants. In the 1980s, 40 percent of men and 60 percent of women reported using one or more medications every forty-eight hours; 20 million people used marijuana daily. In 1981, one in six high school seniors tried cocaine.

The family, once an oasis of love and nuturance, has itself become a battleground. An estimated 6 million women are abused by their husbands or boyfriends every year—the leading cause of injury to women has become physical assault by a spouse or partner—and from 2,000 to 4,000 die as a result of their injuries. The nation's police spend about one-third of their time responding to domestic violence calls. Child abuse is also on the rise. Reported cases doubled between 1976 and 1981 to 851,000 and continued rising throughout the 1980s. Unreported cases of child abuse or neglect are estimated to be another 5 million.

These trends, driven by a diet too high in animal food and an overly materialistic world view, are part of an overall spiritual separation from tradition and a collapse of fundamental human relationships. If they are not reversed, these trends could lead to the widespread collapse of communities, nations, and civilization itself.

Destruction of the Environment

The destruction of the environment is being driven in part by the delusion that nature can be conquered or exploited without cost. It is also being driven by misguided priorities including the short-term quest for material gain while ignoring the long-term consequences. Let us look at the scope of this increasingly critical problem.

There are 4.5 million known toxic chemicals, and 375,000 new chemicals are being produced annually. In the United States, chemical production increased 67 percent between 1967 and 1977. Most chemicals have never been tested or certified as safe. Pesticides, polychlorinated biphenyls (PCBs), heavy metals, and other residues accumulate in fatty tissue as they move up the food chain. By the time they reach humans, their concentration may have increased a million times. Each year, one ton of chemical wastes is produced per capita in the United States, and most of it is released into the environment or disposed of illegally.

Meanwhile, industrialization has produced great increases in atmospheric carbon dioxide, lead, sulphur dioxide, and other chemicals, leading to widespread air pollution, smog, and acid rain. Atmospheric concentrations of carbon dioxide have increased by 25 percent since 1958, mostly as a result of burning oil and coal. The United States and the Soviet Union now account for 45 percent of the worldwide emissions of CO_2.

Pollution of the atmosphere could create a greenhouse effect, raising global temperatures, triggering massive climatic changes, and submerging seacoasts. Agriculture, food processing, and food transportation contribute directly and indirectly to this problem. For example, 65 percent of automobile pollution comes from trips to the supermarket.

The world's oceans, lakes, and waterways are being increasingly polluted from oil spills, chemical run-offs, pesticides, PCBs, industrial pollutants, heavy metals, and sewage. Ninety percent of the pollutants remain in the coastal waters, though ocean currents do transport chemical residues worldwide; high levels of DDT, for example, have turned up in the fat of Antarctic penguins.

In 1950, 30 percent of the world's land surface was covered by forest. In 1975, tropical rain forests and woodlands declined to

Biodiversity and the Rain Forest

Biodiversity, or the proliferation of plant and animal species, offers an interesting example of the effect of climate and environment on life on Earth. Biodiversity is primarily a function of the upward, expanding energy produced by the rotation of the Earth. Earth's centrifugal force is strongest at the equator, and it is in the equatorial zones that biodiversity is the greatest. For example, it is estimated that one-half of all plant and animal species on the Earth live in the equatorial rain forests. Tropical rain forests contain up to 80 percent of the world's land vegetation and provide a substantial amount of the planet's oxygen. Heaven's more yang, contracting force reduces biodiversity, so the range of plant and animal species decreases as we move north and south toward the poles, where this centripetal force is strongest.

The predominance of yin, centrifugal energy at the equator produces a fragile ecosystem in the rain forest.

Ninety-five percent of the nutrients are held above the ground in plants, rather than below the ground in the soil. By contrast, the soil in temperate zones (where heaven's force is stronger) retains a large percentage of the nutrients below the surface in topsoil. Because a rain forest is so fragile, once its vegetation is cut, its soil is less able to regenerate itself. Every year, 100,000 square kilometers of rain forest are cut and destroyed (an area equal in size to Switzerland and the Netherlands). It is estimated that these activities have already reduced the world's rain forests by 55 percent of their original area.

One species of plant is currently vanishing each day due to the spread of modern civilization. About 20 to 40 animals depend on each plant. At the present rates, 130 species of animals will become extinct each day by the end of the century, and one-quarter of all animal species now existing will disappear by the mid-twenty-first century. Since large tracts of the rain forest are being cut to make room for grazing livestock and for growing livestock feed, a large-scale shift to the direct consumption of grains, beans, and other vegetable-quality foods could substantially reduce the destruction of this precious resource and help preserve priceless plant and animal species that took millions of years of natural evolution to appear on Earth.

12 percent, and by 2000, they are expected to shrink to 7 percent. Logging, mining, and cattle ranching are major causes of deforestation. The loss of crop lands and depletion of water reserves are also increasing. Twenty-eight percent of the world's land is suffering from drought, and by the middle of the twenty-first century, one-third of the remaining farmland could be lost to artificial encroachment of the desert. In Africa, planting huge tracts of a single crop, overgrazing, deforestation, and poor irrigation have resulted in chronic droughts and famines.

In the United States, one-third of the farmland has declined in productivity because of erosion. One inch of topsoil takes from 100 to 2,500 years to develop naturally and can be destroyed by modern farming techniques in 10 years. Water tables are dangerously low in many parts of the country from excessive agricultural irrigation. Seventy percent of global water is being used to irrigate new "miracle crops," produced with artificial fertilizers and sprays. The modern meat-centered diet is a major contributor to this problem; for example, one pound of meat requires 6,000 gallons of water to produce, while one pound of wheat requires only 60 gallons. Modern civilization seems to be at war with the environment. However, if peace is not declared—and declared soon—humanity may find itself on a harsh and largely uninhabitable planet.

TOWARD ONE PEACEFUL WORLD

As you can see, humanity has far to go before we can realize the beginning of a new era. Assuming that we are able to prevent a full-scale nuclear war, the challenges ahead of us are many; let us take a closer look at them. Dividing the 120 years from 1982 to 2102 into six 20-year periods, we can trace the progression of this epochal transformation in more detail.

Period 1 (1982 to 2002): World Health and Ecology

The development and spread of the natural foods movement in the 1960s and '70s paved the way for a new awareness of diet and preventive health care in the 1980s. Macrobiotic and holistic approaches gained increasing recognition during that decade, in addition to support by doctors and medical researchers. Through the 1990s, as the influence of natural and macrobiotic health care continues to spread, we will begin to correct the general negative tendencies in the domains of food, agriculture, and medicine. The importance of a naturally-balanced diet in preventing disease will start to gain recognition throughout society, and modern medicine and science will begin to discover the role of ki, or energy, as well as those of the mind and emotions, in health, healing, and human life. Preventive strategies involving a balanced diet and ecological living will begin to reverse the decline of physical and psychological health and will reform destructive agricultural practices. The connection between the modern diet and the destruction of the Earth's environment will become more apparent, prompting many people to shift to an ecologically balanced way of eating.

Period 2 (2002 to 2022): World Economy and Social Structure

As ecologically sound agricultural practices and holistic, macrobiotic approaches to health care continue to be implemented, newer, more constructive economies will emerge based on cooperation with, rather than exploitation of, nature. Medicine, for example, will begin to rely less on drugs and more on diet and daily life, and dietary recommendations will extend beyond the prevention of disease to the actual recovery from chronic disease. The connection between diet and the mind will become more clearly understood, leading to the application of holistic models to the prevention and correction of social problems such as crime, drug abuse, and family violence. The family will start to be restored as the center of society, and communities will provide support and encouragement to all of their members. Preserving the environment will replace the arms race as the leading priority among nations, leading to increased global cooperation and understanding. The wide-scale shift to a grain-bean-and-vegetable-based diet will save tremendous amounts of energy and provide a permanent solution to world hunger. During this time, humanity could experience encounters with extraterrestrial intelligence, leading to a re-evaluation of the current concepts in science, medicine, and human history and prompting the further study of astronomy and cosmology. Archeological and ancient world studies may also provide clear evidence of a unified world civilization that existed in the past.

Period 3 (2022 to 2042): World Science and Industry

A second industrial revolution will begin, prompted by the development and perfection of atomic transmutation. Chemistry and physics will discover the spiral unity of life and change their conventional theories based upon the new understanding that atoms are constantly changing from one to another under normal atmospheric conditions, with low temperature, pressure, and energy. As the technology of transmutation is applied to industry on a world scale, the materials necessary for human prosperity will become available in practically unlimited quantities and at low cost. These developments will render obsolete the competition for natural resources and raw materials and will pave the way for the discovery of unlimited natural sources of energy, such as electromagnetic energy or ki. Science will begin to serve humanity and will become unified with philosophy.

Period 4 (2042 to 2062): World Philosophy and Consciousness

The developments in astronomy, history, and cosmology experienced in Period 2 coupled with social and economic changes will usher in a new concept of universal origin and spirit. Refined on a social level, this universal metaphysical sense will dissolve the barriers of traditional cultural and religious separation, creating a one-world, planetary consciousness and a general sense of universal spirituality. Families will gain an increased awareness of their spiritual origins and ancestral traditions and will transmit this awareness to their children. As the rigid borderline between spirit and matter dissolves, people will gain an intuitive awareness of eternal life and the world of spirit.

Period 5 (2062 to 2082): World Travel and Politics

With the advent of natural transmutation, natural energy, and other new sciences, together with the new cosmology and spiritual insight, active worldwide transportation and space travel will commence. Human civilization will begin to extend beyond the Earth and into the solar system, opening the door to a new era of human development. A one-world language may also develop and, together with active transportation and communication, will finally dissolve all the barriers of national sovereignty, ushering in a totally new concept of politics. Passports and visas will finally become things of the past.

Period 6 (2082 to 2102): World Government

During this last period, all these developments will merge, further refining and unifying all our new discoveries. Humanity will experience the realities of its new civilization and pass through the final maturing process, learning to maintain and administrate its civilization through a new world government. Let us consider what this new world government will be like.

THE GOVERNMENT OF THE FUTURE

There was at one time, long before what is now called recorded history, a civilization in which all people were unified under one peaceful world government. This planetary civilization was lost to various catastrophes and doesn't appear in our history texts or conscious knowledge. But deep inside, humanity has never lost its memory of that civilization and has nurtured the memory—in the form of an aspiration toward one world—through the thousands of years of war, conflict, and struggle that we call recorded history.

In ancient Greece, the wellspring of Western civilization, Plato's *Republic* discussed a proposal for a new world political structure that would be governed by universal law as interpreted by a "philosopher king," rather than by artificial law and material power. Other writers and thinkers have presented various proposals: *The Discourse of Eternal Peace* by Immanuel Kant; *Utopia* by Thomas Moore; *The City of the Sun* by Tommaso Campanella; *Erewhon* by Samuel Butler. Saint Augustine proposed a world society managed according to Catholic principles, a global nation of God.

In the Old Testament, the prophet Isaiah saw a vision of a future world with no sickness or hostility; and in the book of Revelation, Saint John the Divine saw a similar vision of the "new Jerusalem," in which all nations would be healed by the leaves of the Tree of Life. In other words, these prophets foresaw that at some time, humanity would manage its affairs by the laws of the universe or the principles of life and would not need the artificial inventions of man's law and power.

None of these visions or proposals, however, has been realized or fulfilled. In fact, sickness, war, hostility, and conflict have only continued to escalate with the advent of modern technology. In the twentieth century, the League of Nations, the United Nations, and the World Federalist Movement arose to address these problems. However, as with earlier proposals and attempts, they have not provided effective long-term solutions.

So far, we have seen many attempts to discover the ideal way of organizing society. Every method involves polarizing society into two complementary groups—the "governing" and the "governed." For example, monarchy and feudalism, in which single individuals govern large numbers of people, have often been followed by various forms of democracy, which have in turn given rise to different versions of bureaucracy, in which small groups of people govern the rest, as in the United States and the Soviet Union.

What is the most natural social organization? The family. The family is the most natural, time-tested self-governing unit within all human society. Order is very easily and naturally established in the family: parents guide their children because they have more experience and therefore more knowledge and a wider view. Children automatically respect their parents, and parents automatically love and care for their children. When a child becomes sick, his parents can't sleep; they stay up all night at the foot of the child's bed, worrying, watching, really selflessly caring about the child. This is all very natural.

Today, of course, this natural structure is collapsing everywhere; families are disintegrating, and people are saying that this type of structure is arbitrary or obsolete. Why is this? Of course, there are many factors involved, but there is one central issue: families are no longer sharing the same food. Food unites the family. After a hard day's work, everyone returns home in the evening. Why? Because they need to eat. Of course, sex is there too, but food is more urgent; everyone needs to eat every day, two or three times a day. As long as everyone continues eating together, the basis for family unity remains. If that basis collapses, the family will collapse.

Suppose everyone eats at a different restaurant and then comes home to sleep. This is not a family, but simply a hotel. Including sex, maybe it's a motel. But it's not a family.

If the whole family eats together, but if its food is not selected and prepared with a good understanding of what effects it can have on health and peace of mind, what will happen? The family members may stay together since they are eating together, but they will also argue and fight constantly or gradually alienate themselves because of deteriorating health.

In other words, to maintain a unified, happy, peaceful family, there must be some central person providing all the family members with the correct biological foundation for their health and happiness through proper nourishment. All the family members will then naturally orient themselves around that person; the children's love and respect will be naturally there, without being artificially taught, and the parents will naturally want to love and care for their children.

When families eat this way, and then communities and nations as a whole begin to eat this way, the whole world will begin to think in family terms, and the planetary family of humanity will begin to emerge.

In such a family society, government would not need to enforce certain behavior with power, through various codes, laws, military, police, and courts, as it presently does. This new government would be less a power or police organization and more a service or educational organization. It would provide people with information about how to manage agriculture, industries, education, and so forth, and would consider solutions to any problems that might arise.

The people who would be able to make such evaluations and educate in such a way do not exist in our present-day governments. That is why "politics" has come to be such a low, dirty word. We need to eventually replace this government-by-power with a governing body that can evaluate and judge. In other words, we need a new type of world leader.

Who should be the new world leaders? Who are the most respected people? In a natural family, the oldest members are the wisest and most respected. Today, of course, many senior citizens suffer from chronic illnesses, but they still have more life experience than younger persons do. If our elders were nourished with a better diet, then their consciousness would become very broad, clear, and high.

To manage the affairs of our world family society, we need law—not artificial, arbitrary human laws, but real law: natural, absolute law that is invincible and universal. That law is, of course, the law of change, or the eternal process of change according to yin and yang. World government of the future must be able to apply this invisible order efficiently and accurately to any situation. Practically speaking, we would need an interpreter of the order of the universe and its countless applications and appearances in all of society's affairs.

For this interpreting function, ancient agricultural societies created a council of elders, a gathering of the wisest people among them, people with good health, spiritual awareness, and high consciousness. The day may not be far off when world governing by such a gathering of people is a reality. The government of the future will not be created by any secret, complicated teaching, or through higher education or political theories. The government of the future is being created right now, by our daily practice of eating good food, by our study of yin and yang, by our respect for our elders and love for our juniors, and by the growing happiness and health of our families. From these simple beginnings, we will definitely be able to realize humanity's long cherished dream of one happy, peaceful world.

When we finally arrive at the year 2102, it will not be called 2102. It will be called Year One, the first year of the new era of humanity, according to the new world calendar. This calendar will reflect all the great traditions of cosmological understanding, composed from our new world cosmology and written in our new world language. The same as Stonehenge, the *I Ching*, and the Aztec and Mayan calendars, it will provide astronomical and meteorological information for planting and harvesting. It will gauge the periods of change and rest, of forward progress and inward reflection. Charting the turning of the cosmos and the stirrings of the Earth, the new world calendar will assist us as we create, change, and recreate the affairs of humanity, playing day and night as one planetary family within this infinite universe.

For Further Study

For those who wish to study further, the Kushi Institute of the Berkshires, an educational institution originally founded in Boston in 1979, offers full- and part-time instruction for individuals who wish to become macrobiotic teachers and counselors. It also presents seminars and programs for anyone interested in learning about the macrobiotic way of life. The following two seminars may be of special interest to the readers of *Other Dimensions:*

Studies of Destiny. In these ongoing seminars presented at the Kushi Institute of the Berkshires, Michio Kushi explores many of the topics discussed in this book. Included are fascinating and revealing studies of the way to see, judge, and freely manage your personal destiny—and the destiny of planet Earth—based on yin and yang, the *I-Ching*, 9 Star Ki and Oriental astrology, and the art of physiognomy. These residential seminars include macrobiotic/vegetarian meals.

Spiritual Training Seminars. These ongoing seminars presented at the Kushi Institute of the Berkshires are part of a progressive series designed to enhance each person's capacity for self-realization and -fulfillment. They feature practice and experience, and include studies of reincarnation and the spiritual world, *The Gospel According to Thomas,* and the teachings and prophecies of Buddha, Jesus, and Nostradamus, as well as meditation, prayer, and chanting for health and peace. *Spiritual Training Seminars* are residential and feature simple macrobiotic/vegetarian meals.

For more information about these and other macrobiotic resources and programs, contact:

The Kushi Institute
Box 7
Becket, Massachusetts 01223
(413) 623-5742

For Further Reading

Michio Kushi has authored a wide variety of books that deal with topics such as those presented in *Other Dimensions*. The following titles are especially recommended for further reading:

Kushi, Michio. *The Book of Do-In*. Tokyo: Japan Publications, 1979.

Kushi, Michio. *On the Greater View: Collected Thoughts on Macrobiotics and Humanity*. Garden City Park, NY: Avery Publishing Group, 1987.

Kushi, Michio, with Stephen Blauer. *The Macrobiotic Way: The Complete Macrobiotic Diet & Exercise Book*. Garden City Park, NY: Avery Publishing Group, 1985.

Kushi, Michio, with Edward and Wendy Esko. *The Gentle Art of Making Love: Macrobiotics in Love and Sexuality*. Garden City Park, NY: Avery Publishing Group, 1990.

Kushi, Michio, with Alex Jack. *The Book of Macrobiotics*. Tokyo: Japan Publications, 1986.

Kushi, Michio, with Alex Jack. *One Peaceful World*. New York: St. Martin's Press, 1986.

Kushi, Michio, with Phillip Janetta. *Macrobiotics and Oriental Medicine*. Tokyo: Japan Publications, 1990.

Kushi, Michio, with Aveline Kushi and Alex Jack. *Food Governs Your Destiny*. Tokyo: Japan Publications, 1990.

Kushi, Michio, with Olivia Ordeson. *Macrobiotic Palm Healing: Energy at Your Fingertips*. Tokyo: Japan Publications, 1989.

About the Authors

Michio Kushi was born in Kokawa, Wakayama-ken, Japan, in 1926. He devoted his early years to the study of international law at Tokyo University. Following World War II, he became interested in world peace through world government and met Yukikazu Sakurazawa (known in the West as George Ohsawa), who had revised and reintroduced the principles of Oriental philosophy and medicine under the name "macrobiotics." Inspired by Ohsawa's teaching, he began his lifelong application of traditional macrobiotic thinking to modern world problems.

In 1949, Michio Kushi came to the United States to pursue graduate studies at Columbia University. Since that time, he has lived in this country and lectured throughout the United States, Canada, Eastern and Western Europe, Japan and other parts of Asia, Australia, and South America. He is the founder of Erewhon, a pioneer distributor of natural foods; *East West Journal*, a monthly magazine dealing with holistic health and ecology; and *Order of the Universe*, a journal of philosophy and science. In 1978, he founded the Kushi Institute, an educational center for the training of macrobiotic teachers and health counselors, headquartered in western Massachusetts with affiliates throughout the world. He has published a number of bestselling books, including *The Book of Macrobiotics*, *The Cancer Prevention Diet*, *The Macrobiotic Way*, and *One Peaceful World*.

Michio Kushi currently lives in Brookline and Becket, Massachusetts, with his wife, Aveline, also a leading voice in macrobiotic education. His ongoing activities are reported in the quarterly newsletter *One Peaceful World*, published by the Kushi Institute of the Berkshires.

Edward Esko helped pioneer macrobiotic education in North America during the 1970s. He began studies with Michio Kushi in 1971 and for the past seventeen years has taught macrobiotic philosophy, health care, and related subjects throughout the United States and Canada, as well as in Western and Eastern Europe, South America, and Japan. He has lectured on modern health issues at the United Nations in New York and is on the faculty of the Kushi Institute of the Berkshires. He has co-authored or edited several popular books, including *Natural Healing Through Macrobiotics, Doctors Look at Macrobiotics, The Gentle Art of Making Love,* and *The Macrobiotic Approach to Cancer.* He lives with his wife, Wendy, and their seven children in Becket, Massachusetts.

Index

Photograph Credits

Photo on page 32 from the UFO Photo Archives, Tucson, Arizona.

Photo on page 56 from the UFO Photo Archives, Tucson, Arizona.

Photo on page 123 from the Mary Evans Picture Library, London, England.
   Credit: Mary Evans/Andrew Green.

Photo on page 124 from the Mary Evans Picture Library, London, England.
   Credit: Mary Evans/Harry Price Collection, University of London.